EVERYONE NEEDS SUSTAINABILITY

How everyone can make a difference

TED SCHIERER

Published by JETT Publishing

8350 EP True Parkway Unit 1301
West Des Moines, Iowa 50266

All Scripture quotations, unless otherwise noted, are from the Holy Bible, New International Version © 2011 Biblica, Inc.

First Edition, 2014

ISBN: 9780692372302

Printed in the United States of America

Comments on *Everyone Needs Sustainability*

Doug Carter, Senior Vice President of EQUIP "Thank you for your vision and passion around the issue of sustainability... in terms of the betterment of communities, you are to be applauded for your heart in this arena."

Alex Tuckness, Professor, Department of Political Science, Iowa State University Everyone Needs Sustainability "is a sincere plea to the reader to realize the perils of unsustainability and the greater joy we find when embrace sustainability as a lifestyle."

Pam Tripp, CEO, CommWell Health "Ted Schierer provides a mind, body, soul approach to addressing man made challenges with proactive solutions that create sustainability. Everyone Need Sustainability allows the reader to examine our world through innovation and creativity, beckoning us to become good stewards of what God created and entrusted to us."

Rick Christman, Assistant Provost, Ohio Christian University "I believe it is the responsibility of educational institutions to provide a clear purpose for service, both academically and experientially, embedding an understanding within our students that service is everyone's responsibility, to give of ourselves for the betterment of individuals and the greater community. This is one of the foundational premises of *Everyone Needs Sustainability*."

Wes Saade, MD, Total Care Family Medicine "When health is not sustainable, early death is the ultimate result. *Everyone Needs Sustainability* links personal sustainability with personal health including how our lifestyle, values, and thinking affect us physically."

Dedication

This book is dedicated to:

My father, Robert Schierer, who sacrificed for us and has been a constant support. He was a rock and a shelter in our family's biggest storm.

It is also dedicated to people that want to make a difference in the community with their unique set of interests, experience, skills, and abilities, and to the mentors of the world who do the hard work of facilitating lasting life change. You are the leaders who build sustainable community. Everyone is needed.

Table of Contents

Foreword

In a world where everything has a "Shelf Life"...Humans have gotten really good at living a "Disposable Life." We have to have the latest tech tool in our hands or in our homes. The result? Nine million tons of e-waste generated per year[1], and 250 million tons of municipal solid waste per year[2] in the U.S. alone.

And what of God's love for us? Many have experienced, through various religious teachings, that we have an angry and vengeful God. That we better not "make God mad" because "He's keeping score." Fortunately, Christ teaches us that legalistic rules are not the passion of our Father at all. Unconditional Love is all God has for us.

In *Everyone Needs Sustainability*, Ted Schierer pours out his Passion for Christ and sustainability. "Nothing can free us more than unconditional acceptance. This is why divine love is the most important love." That notion of Divine love changes everything for mankind. *Everyone Needs Sustainability* gives us the "blueprint" to live an eternal life with our Father...through the love of Jesus and specific ways we can make a difference in our communities to help them become more sustainable. It's a must read for the head...and the heart.

J. Michael (Mac) McKoy, Radio host of "Restoring Hope, Live."

[1]Bora, K. (2013, December 16). Used Electronics Don't Die: New E-Waste World Map Reveals Worldwide Toll Of Discarded Electronics. International Business Times.

[2]Municipal Solid Waste Generation, Recycling, and Disposal in the United States: Facts and Figures for 2012. (n.d.). Retrieved August 12, 2014, from http://www.epa.gov/solidwaste/nonhaz/municipal/pubs/2012_msw_fs.pdf

Acknowledgements

Thanks to:

Nathan Eckel and his team: For introducing me to new concepts including writing a book, excellent feedback on writing and process, and for facilitating personal growth.

Ryan Larimore and Alex Tuckness: For efficient and excellent editing work; your feedback was invaluable.

Parents: For Dad's example of generosity to family and community service through Kiwanis and Juanita's dedication to her family.

Lutheran Church of Hope: For being an example of a church making a big difference in the community through volunteer service and for providing an excellent growth community.

Mentors: The material in this book was influenced and inspired by a wide variety of excellent scholars and teachers including their books, podcasts, websites, and audio material. The new creation material was based on the work on N. T. Wright and Eben Alexander. The divine intimacy, covenant relationship, and community outreach material was influenced and inspired by the work of Tim Keller. The material on Christian purpose and personal sustainability was based on the teaching and writings of Rick Warren and John Baker and several teaching series at Saddleback Church. No one is better at applying teaching himself and helping others apply it than John Maxwell. His personal growth plans are based on practical daily disciplines and his example in leadership provides a model for implementing change.

Suggested Reading

Alexander, E., *Proof of Heaven*

Bradshaw, J., *Healing the Shame that Binds You*

Brown, B., *Daring Greatly*

Collins, J., *Good to Great*

Collins, J., and Hansen, M. *Great by Choice*

Corbett, S., and Fikkert, B. *When Helping Hurts*

Goleman, D., *Emotional Intelligence*

Gladwell, M., *Outliers*

Gladwell, M., *What the Dog Saw*

Keller, T., *Center Church*

Keller, T., *Generous Justice*

Keller, T., *Meaning of Marriage*

Keller, T., *Prodigal God*

Maxwell, J., 21 *Irrefutable Laws of Leadership*

Maxwell, J., 15 *Indisputable Laws of Growth*

Oberbrunner, K., *The Deeper Path*

Oberbrunner, K., *Your Secret Name*

Ortberg, J., *Soul Keeping*

Randers, J., *2052*

Rath, T., *Strengths Finder 2.0*

Royte, E., *Garbage Land*

Swanson, E., and Williams S. *To Transform a City*

Warren, R., *Purpose Driven Life*

Warren, R., Amen, D., and Hyman, M. *Daniel Plan*

Wright, N.T., *Surprised by Hope*

Wright, N.T., *After You Believe*

Introduction

This book attempts to make the case for prioritizing community involvement. Community involvement can occur through volunteer organizations, family to family contacts, peer to peer contacts, businesses, non-profit organizations, governmental organizations, and combinations of these.

Community involvement must be a priority because:

- It is key to personal and family sustainability. If we and our families are not outward focused, individualism and isolation lead to self-destructive behaviors that have cumulative effects on the community. Outward-focused individuals and families are sustainable and balanced. Personal sustainability forms the foundation upon which all other areas of sustainability are based. If people are not personally sustainable, they will be driven by consumption standards in consumer cultures.

- Communities will not remain sustainable long-term if those who give back to the community are outnumbered significantly by those who do not. Communities are designed to function best when the maximum number of people are involved in helping others within their own neighborhoods. Government responsibility for those in need has not had a good track record. This approach lacks the kind of community that helps people become self-sustaining. In contrast, outreach to the community helps us while we help others.

- National financial sustainability is currently dependent on economic growth instead of active management of the debt. Economies that depend on fixed natural resources in order to grow will eventually stop growing when the physical resources become cost prohibitive or run out. If resources become scarce or there is a prolonged depression, debt will become unsustainable unless it is managed. When people get involved in changing lives in the community, it produces more taxpayers and more financial responsibility. Personal sustainability is one of the few ways to address financial sustainability in the midst of uncertain economic fluctuations that are certain to come.

- Environmental sustainability represents the ultimate tipping point; a physical one. If the finely tuned biosphere tips irreversibly, there is no return. As a result, there would be no return for any economy dependent on natural resources for growth. Economies must learn to depend on something other than physical resources such as the sustainability hierarchy of reduce, reuse, and recycle. Sustainable growth can occur within this hierarchy. Renewable energy is an example.

The different types of sustainability listed above are interdependent. Repetition of interdependent sustainability themes is done to bring awareness to the importance of their interdependence and to reinforce the lessons of interdependence so that we remember them better. Repetition is a key to learning. Repetition in this book expands upon the material in a chapter specific manner. For example, obesity and addiction affect personal, community, and financial sustainability.

The impact of obesity and addiction on personal well being is discussed in Chapter 1 whereas the financial implications are expanded upon in Chapter 3.

What do we need to learn about sustainability? If there was only one lesson that everyone could take away from this book, it would be that we need everyone to do their part to better the community. Communities were originally designed by the Creator to depend on this kind of involvement and interaction. The more involved citizens become in their community, the more sustainable the community becomes. In the end, everyone doing their part is what long-term sustainability requires.

Perspective

The material in this book should provide perspective on how we would work together to make a difference in the community. I come from a Christian perspective. However, I am writing about sustainability and forming sustainability groups on the basis of shared concerns, not religious requirements. Any sustainability gathering involving a general audience is focused on common sustainability issues and sensitive to the beliefs and values of others. People of all faiths and those without religious beliefs can work together. Sustainability is a set of complex and widespread issues that is bringing us together in spite of our differences.

I write this from a Christian perspective because faith became the central personal sustainability issue for me. I share my own weaknesses and failures and how faith helped me through those issues. I have learned more from the experience of other people than by any other means. If you are not a person of faith, these chapters or sections are not intended to offend. If they seem shocking at times, they were shocking to me too at one time.

I approach faith from the perspective that the Bible has proven itself to be the Word of God over and over throughout the generations in spite of the criticism it has received. For example, critics at one time denied the existence of cities and people in the Bible for which direct archaeological evidence was later found. The central message of the Bible remains untainted in spite of minor errors. I do not hold a fundamentalist view of the Bible or creation because those views do not fit well with the available evidence. I do not intend to come across as too authoritative but simply try to reflect the relational realities God brought into my life and their relevance to sustainability. In terms of defending issues of faith with scholarly evidence, other resources like NT Wright's 3 volume series *Christian Origins and the Question of God* and Josh McDowell's *Evidence for Christianity* have already done this.

The following is an attempt to help those without religious beliefs or those of different faiths to gain perspective on difficult matters. The Bible is a very uncomfortable book at times for anyone who encounters it. Sometimes it tells a shocking story because it does not avoid the realities of the context of the authors. Sometimes God makes statements that are shocking to get our attention. He even makes Himself look bad at times. All of these uncomfortable occurrences have a purpose. Ultimately, it is to bring us into relationship with Him. For many years, I was annoyed by such things and even hated some of the things I didn't understand and blamed God for wrongdoing. This went on until He revealed who He is to me. When He revealed His loving nature and how much He cares for me, I stopped the prolonged cycles of blaming Him for the difficulties in life that I did not understand. Trials always tempt us to blame someone else. It never helps. We are better off turning to God in trials and confusion, not away.

Be assured that nothing is intended to come across as superior or self-righteous. I'm open about my many weaknesses and failures for this very reason. For example, when I discuss idolatry in the Divine Love chapter, it is from a perspective of attempting to facilitate closer relationship with God, not from a perspective of rules and regulations. This chapter was moved to reduce its shock value for people not of faith.

Personal sustainability is the first chapter because human behavior is the basis of all other types of sustainability.

Humans are very complex. We are influenced by our biology, psychology, sociology, and spirituality. Superficial discussions don't help complex, deeply relational beings. For this reason, the material on personal sustainability, community sustainability, and faith goes deep. This book will be uncomfortable at times. When it becomes uncomfortable, take some time to reflect on what is affecting you.

Chapter 1

Personal Sustainability

Personal Sustainability

I have burned out at least four times in my life. In high school, I was in three sports and burned out of all of them. As an undergraduate, I over-studied and burned out of my classwork. Then in grad school and beyond, I never allowed myself to take a break to fully recharge during years of research and teaching and became burned out of both. Is there a pattern here? As God provided a second chance as a biologist, it was clear that the former unsustainable patterns had to change. I began to take evenings and weekends off. What a novel idea! As a new way of living began to settle in, God broke through spiritually. Instead of wanting to stay in bed, I was getting up on my own and I was refreshed. It was also difficult to go to bed because I was excited about life again. Because I spent so many years living unsustainably, the topic of personal sustainability was very relevant. Personal sustainability is living in harmony with God, ourselves, and others.

What is Burn-out?

Burnout is a pattern of energy mismanagement that leads to the inability to continue in an endeavor or relationship. It involves a physiological component. The energy to continue is missing.

Why Do We Burn Out?

Energy mismanagement is the physiological factor that leads to burn-out. Identity issues cause us to mismanage energy and decisions. We burn out because of unsustainable thinking and living patterns. Energy is wasted by obsessive thinking and behavior patterns about controlling what we can't control. Control issues come from insecurity about what we rely on for our identity. When we react to perceived threats to our identity, those reactions tend to waste energy. For example, some people burn out of relationships because they feel controlled by the other person. People - out of careers because they can no longer deal with a personnel situation out of their control.

Control is our way to cope with fear and resentment. It manifests itself in many different ways. One of my control issues is people pleasing. I stayed in the wrong major trying to please my parents. I assumed that switching would have meant rejection from my family. As it turned out, almost the opposite was true. I stayed in a legalistic church environment for 10 years that was unhealthy for me because I was afraid of displeasing friends if I left. Whenever someone left the church, they were considered to have fallen away from their faith even if they joined a different church. My decisions were fear-based. Eventually, that caught up with me.

The core identity indicators of fear and resentment are also the core energy wasters because our identity determines how we use our energy. Too many unhealthy inputs and too few healthy inputs combine to waste large amounts of energy. If we let fear, resentment, and control predominate our thinking, we will burn out over time. Weak relationships speed up the process, while strong relationships counter the effects of fear and resentment. Weak relationships are characterized by protectionism from vulnerability. Protectionism doesn't work because it denies us the confidence that we are accepted in spite of our flaws. The lack of vulnerability reinforces perfectionistic pressures that we have to hide our flaws as if we need to be perfect in order to be accepted by others. The impossibility of a perfectionistic mindset precludes a healthy acceptance of self and dramatically increases a sense of insecurity. Security is provided only by relationships in which we are vulnerable and still accept ourselves and find ourselves accepted by others. Protectionism puts up defenses that block out the good and the bad, not just the good. The end result of protectionism is that our relational needs are not met because we blocked the kind of vulnerability we need for true security, (Brown, B. *Daring Greatly*). Preventing burn-out requires decreasing fear and resentment and increasing input from healthy relationships.

Why We Choose Unsustainable Paths

Few people would knowingly choose an unsustainable path. The dominant cultural standards create pressures within our societies, and these pressures make it seem normal to pursue a path that is unhealthy. People often feel that they have no choice but to succumb to what cultural norms dictate. I was in this mode of thinking for years. I grew up in a very unstable environment where my parents fought constantly before they divorced when I was in 8th grade. I needed acceptance and thought that throwing myself into academics and sports would help establish a sense of security. I had no idea that those pursuits were slowly becoming my identity, a broken, false identity based on my own performance. I thought that working hard in school and finding a job would establish a sense of safety and stability. This pursuit went on for many years until it wore me out. Performance-based identity issues led to a downward spiral due to energy mismanagement. Year after year, I worked too many evenings and weekends doing work that was a poor fit for me without properly recharging through sufficient quality time away from work. Stage by stage things fell apart.

First, I left research after several years, and then I tried teaching and left it after several years. The entire time, I was filled with insecurity and fear about the future, a constant nagging anxiety in the background that made me feel invalid as a person.

Looking back, I realize that I couldn't take a break because my identity was too dependent on my work. Ironically, my performance identity greatly decreased my ability to perform. In the fall of 2002, things climaxed. My energy had bottomed out, my thinking was confused, and I was not sure I could keep up with my teaching load. I lost my identity, and I was in overwhelming pain. I became suicidal for the first time.

Some common examples of unsustainable paths are listed below:

Job status Sometimes people believe that their job status will lead to the relationships or the recognition that they want. For example, some lawyers burn out of their job because they are overworked in a job they don't like. If they went into it primarily for the job status, they find out that status isn't enough when the job fit is poor.

Marital status Sometimes people get into unsustainable relationships from the cultural pressure to be married by an acceptable age. People fear being left out of social life.

Relationship management People can respond to hurt feelings in unsustainable ways. For example, when we're hurt, we want to respond the way we were treated. We think that will be a quick fix to our hurt feelings. The opposite effect occurs. Hurting others in response to our hurt actually reinforces the negative feelings in us and drives the relationship toward unsustainability. Getting even doesn't bring relief. It's been my natural reaction to hurt for a lifetime and it has never worked.

Addiction   The most common personal recovery issues are eating and porn addictions. For a number of reasons, handling obesity is more complex than instructing individuals to burn more calories than they consume. It is difficult for obese people to get the treatment and environment they need to become healthy. People do not want to label obese people as food addicts because we all know many obese people and it is socially acceptable to over-consume the wrong types of food. Resisting overconsumption is very difficult because the wrong kind of food is continually offered to us by friends, associates, and the marketplace. All of these factors facilitate denial of food addiction. An addiction that is denied cannot be treated.

There is abundant circumstantial evidence that overconsumption of food is a real addiction. Almost all obese individuals indicate that they want to eat less. However, they don't eat less in spite of the negative health and social consequences of obesity. Foods rich in fat and sugar overwhelm the brain's reward system and inhibit the brain's ability to instruct an individual to stop eating. According to Paul Kenny, Associate Professor at the Scripps Research Institute, obesity shares the following characteristics in common with alcohol and drug addiction (Kenny, 2013):

- Obese people develop tolerance (to appetite suppressing hormones).

- Obese people overeat for short-term pleasure, attempt to abstain, and then relapse, the same general pattern observed for drug addiction.
- Weight loss can trigger negative mood and depression in obese people, similar to withdrawal in addicts during abstinence.

- The more obese people eat, the more they want. Obese individuals must increase food consumption to overcome reduced activation of the brain's reward networks.

- Drugs of abuse stimulate the brain's reward systems the way food does.

- It appears that obesity is caused by an overpowering motivation to satisfy the brain's reward centers.

- Endorphin blockers that help reduce heroin, cocaine, and alcohol use in human addicts also reduce food consumption in test subjects.

- Obese rats treated with endorphin blockers display behavior closely related to withdrawal.

- Obese individuals, alcoholics, and cocaine addicts all have low levels of a dopamine D2 receptor.

Obesity is associated with several different health problems, but type 2 diabetes may cause the most significant financial cost. type 2 diabetes is much more common in obese people. Simple carbohydrates have a significant impact on the hormones that regulate fat accumulation. High levels of insulin cause fat to accumulate in fat cells rather than being burned as fuel. Unfortunately, the typical American diet contains about 50% carbohydrates. High amounts of fructose are some of the most concerning simple carbohydrates since they may lead to elevated insulin levels and insulin resistance. Insulin resistance is the hallmark of type 2 diabetes. The best way to reverse this is to decrease the consumption of simple sugars (Taubes 2013).

Sexual addiction The combination of ubiquitous, private access to pornography and ubiquitous dating services could lead to new cultural standards that destabilize marriages that would not previously have been in danger. The appeal of online dating is strong. It gives a false sense of security knowing that thousands of potential matches are easily available. The internet has made it much easier to meet a match with compatible interests, age, and career direction. Internet dating also allows an overemphasis on physical appearance since it is easy to find the exact physical characteristics one is seeking. Unfortunately, this also means that it will always be easy to find someone "better." The pool of millions of online daters ensures that there will always be someone better than the current match and that it will be easy to meet them. What would stop someone from continuing to find a better match? Pain. Eventually, people wear out when a series of relationships fail. We can't keep switching because of the damage produced by each breakup. If the cycle doesn't stop, the damage accumulates until the person runs out of energy.

People that don't stick out the tough times in marriage don't realize the toll it will take on them if they leave for greener pastures. Those who go from marriage to marriage eventually wear out spiritually, mentally, and physically. They burn out relationally, and relational burn-out affects everything else in their life. In fact, relational burn-out leads to life burn-out. Relationship burn-out may lead to far higher numbers of people entering into recovery programs.

Sexual addiction, food addiction, anxiety disorders, and depressive disorders all have increasing impact on personal sustainability, and they can all be addressed by recovery programs. The root cause of all these recovery issues is a broken identity. This is why Celebrate Recovery (CR) can and does address them all. CR creates an environment in which identities can heal through God's unconditional love and a caring community of people who provide accountability without judgment. Recovery programs are a means to address the root causes of all sustainability issues. When people begin living sustainably at the personal level, they can start living sustainably at the community, financial, and environmental levels.

Transition Process from Burn-out to Sustainability

Burn-out can cycle toward cynicism or it can drive us toward sustainable living. If we get sick and tired of being sick and tired, it presents us an opportunity to turn to God. Left to ourselves, the chances of maintaining a healthy, sustainable life are not very good. The Creator knows how the creation works best because He designed it. If we don't seek the Creator's input on how to live, we cut ourselves off from the best source of guidance. His sustainability plan is based on faith, hope, and love, a combination that allows us to manage energy for the long-term (Keller, T. *Every Good Endeavor*). If we don't live according to faith, hope, and love, we tend to burn out in relationships and in life.

Faith, hope, and love are not just good ideas or options. They are essential to living a sustainable life (Wright, N.T. *After You Believe*). Their practical importance is that we burn out if we don't live by them. The Creator designed our minds and lives to work best with the brain chemistry that is produced by faith, hope, and love. Fear and resentment are essentially the opposite of faith, hope, and love and produce the opposite type of brain chemistry. "Sewage water" brain chemistry generated by fear and resentment is not sustainable (Cloud, H. *Boundaries for Leaders*). We face probable burn-out if we live in fear and resentment instead of faith, hope, and love. Dr. Cloud describes in detail the habits and environments that lead to brain chemistry perils and the changes that can renew our minds.

In the midst of my career crisis burn-out, God sovereignly provided a new job as a regulatory biologist. It ended up being a much better fit than teaching, but it definitely didn't seem that way at first. There was a significant learning curve. So much of the veterinary and regulatory material was new and I was convinced that I had made the wrong decision for over a year. During the burn-out period, my addiction to porn returned in full.

It turned out to be a three-year transition period between my teaching job and biologist job before God broke through relationally and brought a sufficient level of sustainability. The next period of life led to turning my life over to God's care. As the learning curve eased in my new job, it was clear that it was a much better fit than teaching and research. God had sovereignly given me a second chance in spite of my poor choices. I could not take the credit and didn't want to. It was the most thankful time of my life. I couldn't help but be thankful for a second chance after so many mistakes.

Before this time, He had been pressing me to get right with Him relationally over and over for at least a year. I felt very distant from God and had significant difficulty connecting to Him and feeling close. Porn had greatly facilitated the distance I put between God and myself. Then, on a vacation, He broke through. I was praying along the Merced River just outside of Yosemite National Park when He pressed me for what seemed like the thousandth time to get right with Him. In frustration, I said "I can't!" because I didn't know what to do. At that exact moment, He provided a direct thought, "I will work with you." This was an answer I had needed all my life. I had never told God "I can't" because I was afraid of what He might do in response. It's actually exactly what He wanted to hear. It was a surrender of my futile attempts to impress Him by being good. His response was exactly what I needed to hear because it clarified that God wanted a relationship, not my performance. His response of "working with me" was inherently relational. God working with me was doable, unlike my former attempts to impress Him. It clarified that I was to depend on a relationship with Him, not my performance. The oppressive weight of performance identity came off because of this foundational relationship with my Creator. There was a peace that He would take care of me through the good times and the bad times, no matter what.

How did I know that He is enough? After an entire year of consistently experiencing God's peace, I knew my relationship with God was going to last. His Presence has never left, even throughout a couple of dark, difficult years. One of the most obvious ways I knew He is enough is that I was truly content for the first time. I didn't need status or popularity to validate my identity. I was content to enjoy the Lord and work an ordinary job for the rest of my life if that's what God wanted.

Another affirmation that He is enough came during a time when I was recovering from the flu in January 2007. I was reflecting on all the changes God had made through His Presence and peace throughout 2006. I felt that I had finally lived a year of real life rather than a life dependent on the approval of others. I felt that I could have died and been satisfied with going to be with the Lord in a much better place, having accomplished little in my earthly life. I no longer needed accomplishments to validate my life. He is enough to validate me. Especially significant was the sense that one good year with the Lord, even one good day or hour after truly coming into relationship with God, was enough to wipe out the emotional past entirely. It was truly an emotional reset experience. The painful parts of my emotional memory had essentially been forgotten even though the cognitive memory was still intact. I no longer lived in chronic emotional pain. The Gospel has infinite power to provide us with an emotional restart no matter our past. This is why there is hope for anyone at any stage of life. The deathbed conversion is a real event even though the loss of a lifetime of fellowship with God is an undeniable tragedy. Most of us run from God much or all our lives thinking He will ruin our lives with legalistic rules and regulations. Nothing could be further from the truth.

We end up with what we reinforce. To live sustainably, we must reinforce faith, hope, and love by dwelling on these things. This breaks unsustainable thinking patterns. Dwelling is the principle of meditation and Scripture memorization (Psalm 1:1-2; 1 Peter 1:4). The opposite results occur if we reinforce fear, resentment, and performance identity. These are all forms of unsustainable thinking.

"....whose delight is in the law of the Lord, and who meditates on his law day and night. That person is like a tree planted by streams of water, which yields its fruit in season and whose leaf does not wither — whatever they do prospers." (Psalm 1:2-3)

"Through these he has given us his very great and precious promises, so that through them you may participate in the divine nature, having escaped the corruption in the world caused by evil desires." (2 Peter 1:4)

"We demolish arguments and every pretension that sets itself up against the knowledge of God, and we take captive every thought to make it obedient to Christ." (2 Corinthians 10:5)

How to Live Sustainably

Faith and trust   Faith and trust in God keep us from wasting energy on fear because we're trusting God to take care of the things outside of our control. I wasted too much energy worrying about getting a permanent job during grad school, postdoc, and my first years in teaching. The burden of this worry is what set me up for a much better alternative. When God offered relationship through the good and the bad times, I wanted it. It was clear that He was revealing who He is so that I would trust Him to take care of the future no matter what.

Hope   Bad news and brokenness should be expected in a fallen world. Is there not a futility in trusting in the cultural standards of a fallen material world? The daily news is probably the strongest evidence that the present earth can't be the last word. We have seen several genocides in the 20th century, 50% divorce rates in many developed countries, a very fragile climate that is tipping, and more. These issues are big enough to make us realize that it doesn't make sense to put our hope in such a broken world. There must be something beyond this earth, and, in Christ, we can look forward to our troubles ending. Unfortunately, they will not end in this life.

This is why Heaven is an essential hope. Because our trials here will not end, we need to hope in God. He will bring our troubles to an end once and for all when he completely renews creation. Hope provides security for the future because of God's promises to make all things right in Heaven. Hope enables us to see everything as an opportunity for God to work (Romans 8:28) because Christ works it out in the end. Hope keeps us from wasting energy on worrying about the future in a broken world.

Love Love is the unconditional acceptance we receive from God and then give to others. Unconditional love is the key to the abundant life (John 10:10) God promises. It is found through total acceptance, not simply striving to be good.

People that receive their unconditional acceptance to a high degree maximize giving and minimize keeping score. As a result, they don't waste very much energy. I wish I was more like those people because the efficiency and effectiveness of their lives is obvious. Receiving and giving love keeps us from wasting energy on guilt, shame, fear, and resentment regarding present and future relationships and circumstances.

Prioritizing and Protecting Our Relationship with God

If God's love is the key to an abundant life, then we need to prioritize and protect our relationship with God. In turn, a healthy relationship with God is the best protection for our identity. Author and pastor John Ortberg has written an entire book dedicated to *Soul Keeping* (2014).

How to Prioritize Our Relationship with God

By establishing a relationship with our Creator   Once a relationship with the Creator is established, an individual has access to the unconditional love upon which a primary identity can be established. A primary identity is one created by God through genetic and biological characteristics, a relationship with Him, and relationships with others. These factors determine who we are and who we become. A primary identity based on the Creator's love establishes a foundation that is not subject to downturns in circumstances or human relationships. If our identities are based only on our own perceptions (self-identity), our performance (performance identity), or the input of our peers (peer-identity), the identity is created within our own minds at a secondary level. The good news is that our primary identity goes deeper and we can redefine our thinking to align with our primary identity. Unless a person believes that there is a Creator who loves them unconditionally, they can't redefine their thinking at a primary level. Their only options are self-identity, peer identity, or performance identity. The possibility of establishing their primary identity still exists but it depends on establishing a relationship with the Creator.

By prioritizing a relationship with God above everything The most important commands in both the Old Testament and the New Testament are summarized by loving God above everything else and loving our neighbor as ourselves. The first four of the Ten Commandments are focused on loving God first. The last six commandments focus on loving our neighbor as ourselves. These were also the greatest commands according to Jesus. Jesus said that the entire Bible is summarized by love God and love neighbor.

The passage on the Ten Commandments is difficult for many. It describes the effects and duration of generational sin and compares that to the abundance of God's grace and mercy. The purpose of the numbers comparison is to indicate that God's mercy and grace is much greater than His discipline so that we may be drawn into relationship with Him. God's discipline is loving in nature because it protects us from ourselves. The Ten Commandments passage also introduces the concept of idols.

What is idolatry Idols are anything we depend on to define us. Idolization is defining ourselves with something or someone other than our Creator. Any of the following can be idols: wealth, status, popularity, sex, family, sports, hobbies, collectables, food, and control. In terms of specifics, we could list millions of idols. Idols are "anything" (v4) we prioritize above God in our hearts.

In the second and third commandments, God commanded that people are to worship Him first. "You shall have no other gods before me. You shall not make for yourself an image (idol) in the form of anything in Heaven above or on the earth beneath or in the waters below" (Exodus 20:3-4). He did this because He wants to protect His relationship with us. Furthermore, verses 5-6 indicate God's relational motive for these commandments by describing His "jealousy" for us and then explaining his desire to show us "love" at a much higher level. "You shall have no other gods before me. (Exodus 20:3, 5, 6)

Idols inhibit our closeness with God. For those who do not have a relationship with God, idols inhibit establishing a relationship with Him until the point they realize that a relationship with God is more important than anything else. Left unchecked, idols lead to unsustainable lives. This occurs due to the pressure associated with depending on circumstances or people outside of our control for our identity.

Commandments 1-4 "And God spoke all these words: 'I am the Lord your God, who brought you out of Egypt, out of the land of slavery. You shall have no other gods before me. You shall not make for yourself an image in the form of anything in Heaven above or on the earth beneath or in the waters below. You shall not bow down to them or worship them; for I, the Lord your God, am a jealous God, punishing the children for the sin of the parents to the third and fourth generation of those who hate me, but showing love to a thousand generations of those who love me and keep my commandments. "You shall not misuse the name of the Lord your God, for the Lord will not hold anyone guiltless who misuses his name. Remember the Sabbath day by keeping it holy. Six days you shall labor and do all your work, but the seventh day is a Sabbath to the Lord your God. On it you shall not do any work, neither you, nor your son or daughter, nor your male or female servant, nor your animals, nor any foreigner residing in your towns. For in six days the Lord made the Heavens and the earth, the sea, and all that is in them, but he rested on the seventh day. Therefore the Lord blessed the Sabbath day and made it holy." (Exodus 20:1-11)

The greatest commandments according to Jesus "Jesus replied: 'Love the Lord your God with all your heart and with all your soul and with all your mind.' This is the first and greatest commandment. And the second is like it: 'Love your neighbor as yourself.' All the Law and the Prophets hang on these two commandments." (Matthew 22:37-40)

By relying on God's love more than anything else

"And so we know and rely on the love God has for us." (1 John 4:16)

By "gazing on the Lord" and "glancing at problems" (Young, S. *Jesus Today*)

"One thing I ask from the Lord, this only do I seek, that I may dwell in the house of the Lord all the days of my life, to gaze on the beauty of the Lord and to seek Him in his temple.' (Psalm 27:4)

How to Protect our Relationship with God

By guarding our hearts with all diligence

"Guard your heart above all else, for it is the source of life." (Proverbs 4:23 HCSB)

By staying far from the edge of sin

"In the paths of the wicked are snares and pitfalls, but those who would preserve their life stay far from them." (Proverbs 22:5)

By protecting our primary identity against identity substitutes
We need to protect our identity from secondary identities
that we have created. We can become so out of touch with
our created (primary) identity that we focus only on an
artificial, secondary identity. It's not our true identity, but
we believe it is. A peer-based identity allows input from
others to define us. A performance-based identity allows
circumstances to define us. Both of these are based on
cultural standards of success and are dependent on our
circumstances.

I defaulted to a performance-based identity for my entire
life. From elementary school through college, my identity
was too dependent on academics and sports. During grad
school, postdoc, and teaching, my identity was too
dependent on research results and teaching performance.
Eventually, it brought me to my knees. It didn't work
because job performance can't replace unconditional
acceptance as the foundation for identity. As Tim Keller
has said, work, marriage or anything other than faith in
Jesus as an identity foundation will "eat you alive" (Keller,
2012). Doesn't this seem a bit extreme? It is not extreme if
the Creator who started and designed life is the source of
life.

"When Christ, who is your life, appears, then you also will
appear with him in glory." (Colossians 3:4)

God protects us mainly by protecting our identity through
a relationship with Himself. He doesn't promise to protect
us from the difficulties of life. Instead, He guarantees that
we will have them in this broken world (John 16:33) and
offers an alternative, His peace (John 14:27). It is as if He is

saying, "It's futile to try and protect yourself. You can't control circumstances or people so trust me instead." If we want protection, the only viable option is to protect our identity in Christ by protecting our relationship with Him. Protecting our identity protects us from whatever is outside our control. We need to protect our relationship with God, because He is our only true protection (Psalm 62 and 91).

"Truly my soul silently waits for God;
From Him comes my salvation.
He only is my rock and my salvation;
He is my defense;

I shall not be greatly moved.
How long will you attack a man?
You shall be slain, all of you,
Like a leaning wall and a tottering fence.
They only consult to cast him down from his high position;
They delight in lies;
They bless with their mouth,
But they curse inwardly. Selah

My soul, wait silently for God alone,
For my expectation is from Him.
He only is my rock and my salvation;
He is my defense;
I shall not be moved.
In God is my salvation and my glory;
The rock of my strength,
And my refuge, is in God.
Trust in Him at all times, you people;
Pour out your heart before Him;
God is a refuge for us." (Psalm 62:1-8 NKJV)

By protecting peace with God   As John Owen, 17th century Vice Chancellor of Oxford University, said, God's peace and strength is the "sum of the promises of grace" (Owen, J. *Mortification of Sin*, Chapter X). Without these, we are blinded from our true identity in Christ. God's peace was the field of hidden treasure for me (Matthew 13: 44). After ten years of medium to high level depression and panic anxiety, there was no doubt for me that life had changed at a foundational level. After the breakthrough at Yosemite, the difference God made was unmistakable, and there was no going back. Since I had been suicidal during my career crisis, peace of mind through Christ was a matter of life and death. It was clear that God's peace was the one thing I could not risk losing.

Most people are afraid of risking cultural standards. God's peace allowed me to risk cultural standards. Cultural idols that conflicted with a relationship with God had to go. After several burn-outs and God breaking through with lasting peace, it was time to put God first. After coming into a relationship with God, a four year period followed in which there was little to no interference in our personal times together. During this period, I didn't feel that I needed much other than getting to know the Lord better. Without question, they were the best years of my life. I was simply happy to be alive and experiencing life without nagging identity fears.

Identity must be guarded with "all diligence" (Proverbs 4:23 NKJV). We must actively guard against our own selfish desires to accept the praise of people as identity security. Identity substitutes of any type are inevitably self-destructive. Peter and the other disciples were very clear about refusing to accept credit for the works of the Spirit partly for this reason (Acts 3:1-16). Internally, we can value the compliments of people without internalizing it as our identity. We must actively refuse to accept the praise of others as an identity substitute. The failure to do this maintenance work weakens and corrupts us.

By establishing personal sustainability boundaries   A boundary is a practical way to take responsibility for attitudes that waste energy. It is a matter of taking control of what we can control (our attitude and actions) and releasing control of what we can't control (the actions of others). Sometimes we let discouragement over what we can't control stop us from acting on what we can control. However, not acting because we don't feel like it reinforces the wrong attitude and ends up wasting more energy. We are more likely to act our way into better attitudes and feelings than waiting for positive feelings to cause us to act. (Maxwell, 2014). Boundaries save us energy by reducing the amount we worry about what we can't control and what does not define us.

Boundaries against fear and resentment   As already discussed, fear and resentment eventually lead to burn-out. The aftershocks of fear and resentment-based actions and words are unsustainable if not addressed. These effects include guilt and shame. If we address the root cause of fear and resentment, we will address guilt and shame. Believing the Gospel and our complete acceptance in Christ is what heals identity.

Boundaries against idolization   Any behavior resulting from idolization is unhealthy and needs a boundary. Self-awareness is required to determine if we are depending on something other than God for our identity needs. If a person can sense fear and resentment, then they will be more able to identify the idol and the behavior. Sometimes we don't realize our behavior is blocking and harming our relationship with God and others. For example, I kept returning to porn rationalizing that a low frequency would not cause harm. It turns out that the frequency didn't matter. Low frequency use has high impact, because idolatry is high impact at any frequency. It had high impact in disrupting closeness with God and others. Porn makes idols out of physical appearance and creates a distorted view of people and relationships. I didn't recognize porn as a problem because I didn't associate it with relationship issues. Most people don't.

Boundaries for daily surrender   Without a daily surrender of dependence on cultural standards, we tend to live in imbalance, moving either too fast or too slow. Living in a state of panic or frozenness is self-destructive and unsustainable. Building an identity on unconditional love is what allows us to go of cultural standards to the point that we can live without them. When we get to that point, we can release the fear and resentment associated with trying to obtain something we have idolized. It's always better to miss out on idols than to self-destruct trying to control or obtain them. Any cultural idol substituted for God leads to self-destruction. This is one of the main reasons God gave us the first four commandments.

Fear and resentment can help us to release control of our idols because these negative feelings help us understand that our idols do not bring us satisfaction. Unfortunately, we don't easily let go of idols because cultural reinforcement keeps them alive in our thinking. We must completely lose confidence in the ability of cultural standards to satisfy us in order to stop returning to them. Burn-out often does the job.

If we are still trying to control an idol, then we have not surrendered it. Successful daily surrender includes releasing all cultural idols as they arise and replacing them with relational sufficiency in Christ. We have to give up on all substitutes for God throughout every day in order to live abundantly. This reflects our fundamental design of being made in the image of God and made to worship Him above everything else. Life breaks down if we don't follow this pattern.

By developing daily disciplines   A faith that acts in spite of feelings and that takes us beyond feelings (Luke 9:23-25) is necessary in a broken world so that we don't compromise the long-term for the short-term. Daily disciplines are God's method for long-term healing (Luke 9:23-25). God does not want an instant character healing for anyone because selfishness can't be removed instantly (1 John 4:16-18). We heal by choosing faith over fear in the context of community on a daily basis (1 John 4:16-18). The following are some practical reasons why we need a faith that is lived out through daily disciplines.

Daily disciplines to protect and strengthen our relationships Faith-based obedience simplifies what feelings tend to overcomplicate, such as obeying the golden rule rather than obeying a relationship scorecard. Many relationships today are in serious trouble because they are based on feelings rather than a covenant before God which has both commitment and feelings (Keller, T. and Keller, K., *Meaning of Marriage*.) As a result, people leave relationships when they fall "out of love."

Daily disciplines to heal us from the damage of idol worship Whenever the personal standard for success is external to the person and based in the material world, the person becomes dependent on externals for happiness and peace of mind. A culturally dependent person is a victim of external circumstances and the actions of others. Victims are easily offended because they become hyper-vigilant about threats or acquisition of cultural standards. I know because I have lived as a victim of externals. It's no fun.

Could it be that looking beyond the black and white of a threat to our identity is an essential tool that God uses to heal us from a misplaced identity foundation? We can catastrophize perceived or actual offenses in a state of hyper-vigilant protection, or we can learn to stop defending an idol that is destroying us. Many, including myself, have struggled with a poverty mindset of holding on to fear and resentment as if it is the only thing that will protect us. Catastrophic thinking has been a survival defense for me. It is based on the false assumption that my defensiveness will actually protect what I think is necessary for survival. However, humans can't thrive on survival thinking. God made people to live in freedom from defending ourselves. The protection mindset blinds us from seeing the abundance of God and the destruction of fear. Whenever we hold onto fear and resentment, we block the flow of grace from God (Mark 11:25).

How can we move from poverty to abundance? Receiving unconditional love and grace and giving it to others is God's method of moving us from a poverty mindset to an abundance mindset. Victims can be unfamiliar with the process of receiving because they are defenders and takers. Instead of receiving freely from God, they take from others to assuage their fears. Giving and receiving does the opposite by satisfying our souls with unconditional love. A satisfied person does not need to take. Realizing that God is enough allows people to let go of defenses such as catastrophic thinking and to replace these defenses with daily disciplines.

Unfortunately, people are leaky. We need to be filled with the Spirit's resources every day to stay satisfied. God designed life on a daily cycle (Luke 9:23-25). We can address our leaks if we make receiving and giving a habit. If that happens, we can move from poverty to abundance, from taking to giving, and from defending to understanding. Replacement works, but only on a daily basis. It is essentially a daily switch from justifying ourselves to gospel justification. If we stop defending ourselves to God, it reinforces that we have received enough love from Him to satisfy us. Conversely, if we defend ourselves, we block awareness of His unconditional love and become takers. We block the source of life by mismanaging our feelings. Daily disciplines are the main way to manage our feelings so that we don't mismanage our energy. Daily disciplines facilitate an even expenditure of energy because they significantly reduce the drama produced by catastrophic thinking. Drama is glorified in the movies, but in reality, it is usually an energy waster that leads to burn-out. This is why daily disciplines are a key to burn-out prevention.

Daily discipline of daily filling God has designed life to be lived on a daily basis. We need a daily filling of unconditional love because our love tanks leak and the fuel gets used up. Filling the love tank doesn't carry over from one day to the next, and emptying it does not carry over to the following day as long as we fill the tank. To maintain a full tank, we need to fix any leaks and fill up the tank daily. Identity issues are like leaks. They need to be fixed in order that we don't waste the fuel. Pouring love into a leaky tank won't provide the permanent fix needed, but love is the best way to help lead people toward divine identity healing. God has to fix the leak through a relationship between Himself and the leaky person. The tank is filled through daily prayer, scripture reading, scripture meditation, fellowship, worship, and discipleship. All aspects of the Christian life contribute to filling the tank. Joshua 1:8 and Psalm 1:2 say to meditate "day and night" on scripture because that practice will fill our love tanks if done in a relationship with God.

If we don't fill our tanks with divine love, our love runs out and we default to cultural standards. This is why God commands us to love Him first. If we don't, we will depend on external factors for attitude, and our attitude will vary with external circumstances or the behavior of others. Viktor Frankl, a survivor of a Nazi concentration camp, said, "Everything can be taken from a man but one thing: the last of the human freedoms–to choose one's attitude in any given set of circumstances" (Frankl, V., *Man's Search for Meaning*). The key to a consistently positive attitude is making the transition from depending on externals for our attitude to depending on internals. As Frankl realized, no one else controls our attitude.

Daily disciplines to prepare us for the unknown Perfectionism is being too afraid to make mistakes in the realm of the unknown. It is not sustainable because it drains energy through performance anxiety and slows the pace of progress. God addresses this issue by giving us faith and hope in His control of life's unknowns. We can trust Him to work through the good times and the bad times simply by knowing who He is. If we trust God's character, we will not fear His handling of circumstances or relationships outside of our control. By this means, Job came to the point of trusting God in spite of losing everything (Job 40: 1-5).

By loving our neighbors as ourselves The scripture is very clear that the quality of our relationships with others affects the quality of our relationship with God. Implicit in 1 John 4:19 is the value of people over the material standards of culture. People are the most valuable part of creation because only souls will pass into the new creation.

Everything material will be remade and renewed. We love our neighbor as ourselves in community. Protecting our relationship with God protects our relationships with others and vice versa. The following are some ways we can practically apply the golden rule.

"We love because he first loved us. Whoever claims to love God yet hates a brother or sister is a liar. For whoever does not love their brother and sister, whom they have seen, cannot love God, whom they have not seen. And he has given us this command: Anyone who loves God must also love their brother and sister." (1 John 4:19)

Loving our neighbors through diverse community An individual can't sufficiently understand an infinite God because of blind spots and limitations. Other people understand different aspects of God's character that we would miss without community. Understanding more aspects of the character of an infinite God, in turn, allows us to become more like Him.

Community is like the industrial inspection process. Multiple inspectors are often needed for one facility. During the inspection, the inspectors help the firm see weaknesses that they were unable to see themselves. Companies need an outside perspective to compensate for their limited viewpoint. Inspectors recognize their own weaknesses and are rotated so that a different pairs of eyes sees the facility according to the rotation schedule. In similar ways, we need others to help us know God and ourselves better. We need a wide variety of perspectives and activities to understand the infinite God at the level that we need to. The activities that increase our understanding of God include fellowship, worship, and discipleship (Warren, R. *The Purpose-Driven Life*).

Loving our neighbors through balanced community
Relationships need a balance of encouragement and
accountability, openness and confidentiality, and many
other paradoxical pairs. Relationships balance opposing
factors. We would wear out if we only experienced one
side of the equation. For example, we need to receive
support for both the successes and failures of life. As Rick
Warren says in the *Preparing for Transformation* podcasts, if
you share a burden in community it is halved, and if you
share a joy or a victory in a community, it is doubled
(Warren, R., 2013).

A healthy community should be people that are neither
needy nor rescuing. People should be comfortable alone
and within their community. When I came into a close
relationship with God, I didn't feel needy when I was
alone. It was good to not be needy, but I didn't understand
the function of healthy community. I felt like I didn't need
people at all. I withdrew from significant aspects of
community. A recent example of balance in this area came
through a good friend. I wasn't there for him in a time of
need. I felt really bad. I apologized to him and he came
back and said, "You know, the neediness is my
responsibility."

Loving our neighbors through accountable community
Celebrate Recovery (CR) is an effective volunteer,
community-based, faith-based recovery program. It is
effective because the bugs have been worked out of the CR
curriculum and processes over the course of more than 20
years (see "About Us" 2014). CR demonstrates how some
people come to church when they are hurting from a life
experience or have finally hit the bottom of a long
unsustainable personal journey. When broken people
follow the program, it yields results. Why? Because CR

addresses the root causes of brokenness in the human heart. CR's core principles are based on healing our identity through establishing a firm foundation of unconditional acceptance. It restores people through a restored relationship with their Creator. The Creator then heals their identity through a daily, lifelong process. CR is an example of the right balance in the difficult area of accountability. When people know that difficult input is coming from people who have been through the same thing, it is clear that it's not condescending. People can accept difficult input when they know it's for their benefit.

Changes that Take Place in a Sustainable Life

In summary, a sustainable life results from establishing a healthy relationship with God and then building healthy relationships with others. Having a relationship with God redeems energy that was formerly wasted on fear, control, and resentment. When our relationship with God is right, we discover our purpose (Warren, R., *The Purpose-Driven Life*). When we discover our purpose, life makes much more sense and tends to flow efficiently.

Action Plan

- Evaluate your relationships with God and others. Are there unhealthy levels of fear and resentment present?

- Memorize scripture for prioritizing and protecting your relationship with God.

- Develop a daily disciplines action plan for your faith and relationships based on the material in this chapter.

- Consider becoming involved in a Celebrate Recovery group to help with identity healing.

48

Chapter 2

Community Sustainability

Everyone Needs Community

Community relationships take us to a higher level in our relationship with God. A community reflects more aspects of God's character, and community relationships require a higher level of unconditional love. We grow the most through our relationship with other people. God designed life to work best when people give to others unconditionally. Humans have a need to love others built into their design so that we can see and understand God's love better. He's a giver. He is also infinite and gives us many different types of love to help us better understand him and other people – including divine love (Chapter 7), brotherly love, passionate love, and covenant love. Other resources have examined more closely these different types of love (Lewis, C.S., *The Four Loves*; Keller, T., The *Meaning of Marriage*).

Without this diversity of loves in community, our love is incomplete. God gives us a fuller, more mature love through working out our relationships over time. As 1 John 4:16-17 says, "This is how love is made complete among us." Completeness is a community process. As I mentioned earlier, I was not adequately aware of the value of community for personal growth. I thought I didn't need people because God was meeting my needs. Eventually, the limitations of isolation became apparent and I had to find a growth community. The wrong kind of community only makes matters worse. It is very important to find a community where there is both nonjudgmental accountability and personal support. We need to keep searching until we find this kind of community. Giving up the search means giving up on the growth we need.

A community helps us grow because each person in our community can see different aspects of our character defects or character strengths due to their own unique set of experiences, character traits, and personality traits. Only a community can get the mentoring job done because each individual is complex. It would be too much for one mentor to address all the character defects in another person. To make matters worse, prosperous, consumer-driven entitlement cultures generate a higher percentage of immature people. Community mentoring may be the only mechanism that will not overload the mentors of the world. In Africa, they say that it takes a community to raise a child, but it's true in any country and in any period of history. We need all the people in our local and wider communities because each person has a unique role in our transformation and sanctification. The Spirit uses each person He brings into our lives to transform and fine-tune our lives. Ephesians 3:17-18 indicates clearly that it is only "together with all the Lord's holy people" that we can "grasp how wide and long and high and deep is the love of Christ." However, every relationship is broken at some level. We need to lower our expectations of people's performance. It is not reasonable, logical, or sensible to expect any person to be more than human. Only God is God; everyone else makes mistakes. For this reason, God expects us to be gracious (Ephesians 4:2; Colossians 3:12-14).

Why Personal Sustainability and Community Sustainability Are Interdependent

Community sustainability comes out of and depends upon personal sustainability. The duration, difficulty, and process of community transformation beginning with individual transformation was described by Eric Swanson and Sam Williams in *To Transform a City* (2010). Our personal goals need to keep the community in mind if the community is to have long-term sustainability. A personal growth journey does not allow for the "we've arrived" mentality. A growth-oriented person doesn't stop when their personal goals are met because their motivation is to include the common good in their journey. Communities need everyone to be continually outward focused.

A healthy, balanced community of friends will not be fooled by us in the long-run. Knowing our friends aren't fooled creates safe accountability and promotes openness. This minimizes the self-imposed pressure of hiding. If we intentionally make ourselves accountable to healthy people, we will grow. In fact, it is impossible to not grow in this kind of atmosphere. People have a tendency to think that they no longer need to grow once they reach a cultural standard or an acceptable level of recovery or maturity because that is what culture tells them. Community protects us from "we've arrived" and keeps us going.

What Is Community Sustainability?

Community sustainability is an interdependent network of families and individuals in a community living personally sustainable lives and working together for the common good.

Adding Value to the Community

Personal sustainability starts with the first commandment, love God (Chapter 1), and community sustainability starts with the second commandment, love your neighbors (Chapter 2, Matthew 22:37-39). In an ideal community, everyone would perform their unique mission within the community. Each person has a unique niche of skills, abilities, experiences, interests, desires, and traits that needs to be applied in the community. As people use their skills in the community, they make it stronger and add value to it. Everyone is important to the health of our communities. God values everyone equally, but he assigns us tasks according to the talents and resources He's given us.

I have a good friend who is a janitor. He is also a good husband and a good leader at Celebrate Recovery. He is very good at sharing his recovery story and recovery lessons with his small group. He has a high level of self-awareness and this provides the depth and clarity needed to help others grow. This is part of what makes him a good leader. He works as a custodian, but he's much more than that. He's linked into the community in several significant ways: through his marriage, through his community group, through large group functions at church, and through Celebrate Recovery. In our culture, it is common to think of a janitor as a "low-value" job. Spiritually, its value can be higher than a "high-impact" job that is performed for selfish reasons. If custodial work is the best fit niche for a person, then that's exactly what they should do and we should see value and blessing in it. My friend makes a difference in the lives of those around him. Being vitally linked into his family, a recovery community, and a healthy church makes him a high impact member of the community, because lives are changing as a result of his input.

Why the Classes Need to Come Together

Human history has patterns and cycles. Throughout history, nations have entered into conflict for a variety of reasons. Those conflicts create adverse conditions for all those involved. However, sacrificial living during times of conflict and struggle has a renewing effect on the lives of a small but influential remnant of people within those societies. This renewing can lead to times of peace and prosperity. Unfortunately, long-term prosperity can eventually lead to a society-wide sense of entitlement, replacing the sacrificial mindset.

Entitlement living ultimately and inevitably leads to a breakdown of community and a return to some level of conflict within and between societies. High levels of entitlement and individualism preclude the type of communities needed to bear each other's burdens. When the disparities between classes become too large, class conflicts arise. Those conflicts worsen over time if the underlying entitlement issues are not resolved. The U.S. experienced some non-violent class wars during the 2008-2009 financial crisis. Busloads of people went to protest outside the homes of CEOs who had filled their pockets while their companies descended into financial ruin (Reich, R., *Aftershock*).

We can look at the patterns in history and address these disparities before unacceptable levels of conflict develop, or we can be passive about or participate in a self-destructive individualism that is crippling the community relationships of prosperous nations and destroying the environment. The U.S. is at the global extreme of the individualism spectrum (Corbett, S. and Fikkert, B., *When Helping Hurts* p. 154) indicating that this level of individualism is destructive. Bringing the classes together to voluntarily share resources and skills helps both sides. It can be argued that sharing resources and skills helps the prosperous people as much as or more than it helps those in need.

Benefits to the Prosperous

Protection from entitlement self-destruction A pertinent issue for the prosperous is that too many are miserable in spite of having met all cultural standards of success. Sharing resources can help keep the prosperous from self-destruction. Giving and service can facilitate personal growth and build relationships. Sharing helps bring greater awareness to what matters most.

Increased national stability The prosperous can lose their prosperity if society itself collapses. The prosperous have far more material wealth to lose if society destabilizes. In Cambodia, the communist revolution took the possessions and lives of its most prosperous citizens (Cormack, D., *Killing Fields Living Fields*). Voluntarily sharing resources is one of the most powerful stabilizers of society. A generous society is a stable one. For most of its history, the United States has been an example of generosity between its citizens. This dynamic changed significantly with the rapid rise of individualism in the economic prosperity following World War II. Wealth distribution through voluntary sharing can return us to higher levels of stability.

Increased international stability If the wealth of skills and resources possessed by Western nations were voluntarily shared in an in-depth and responsible fashion, there would be enough resources to make a significant impact on poverty. This is best done by training citizens of poor countries to provide for themselves, because solving other people's problems from the outside doesn't provide lasting solutions (Corbett, S., and Fikkert, B., *When Helping Hurts*). Organizations such as World Vision and World Relief are excellent examples of self-provision aid. Training for self-provision of basic living needs and well-managed donations of food and other resources reduces the chances that poor countries will destabilize in response to poverty issues (see "Giving," www.worldvision.org and "Microfinance," www.worldrelief.org).

Increased workplace productivity Any organization with multiple employees from small to large would benefit from the recovery principles of Celebrate Recovery because these principles deal with the root causes of conflict that inevitably arise in any organization. The potential savings in workplace productivity from dealing with conflict are enormous.

Benefits to the Poor

Protection from entitlement self-destruction The protection from self-destruction is just as great of a benefit to the poor as it is to the prosperous. Receiving aid with gratitude contributes to an attitude of responsibility. Receiving in a spirit of entitlement can contribute to a lack of personal recovery, lack of responsibility, and remaining in poverty. Giving back to the assisting organization as a volunteer helps the aid recipient.

Material needs Every major city has a network of food banks and good-will donation centers such as the Salvation Army. This can be expanded and enhanced with the skills and resources of the prosperous investing in established organizations. Partnerships are much more efficient than reinventing the wheel. This is true for each area listed below.

Self-provision skills training Non-profits and other organizations with pre-existing self-provision training programs, such as World Vision and World Relief, can use donated resources optimally since they already have successful programs in place. There is great reward and satisfaction in knowing that donations have been invested wisely. Organizations with a track record will continue to make positive change in the community and the world.

Educational opportunities A great diversity of educational organizations exist to help the disadvantaged. Colleges have an excellent track record of making good use of funding in the sciences and other areas. Primary and secondary schools have the greatest need for donations. Money alone isn't effective. It is when the investors also invest themselves in the recipients of the funds that dramatic change is possible.

In 1987, Oral Lee Brown invested her money and time in an entire first grade class at Brookfield Elementary School in East Oakland, California. She made a commitment to put the class through college and she did. Year after year, she invested the time and resources necessary to ensure that her students did their best. Nineteen of the original 23 students went to college (Freudburg, D., 2005).

Counseling and recovery resources Celebrate Recovery is the most effective personal recovery program available on an international scale. It addresses the root cause of unsustainable lives — identity issues (See "About Us," 2014). It is a mostly volunteer organization, but funding would help hire staff and supply recovery resources and recovery centers to those in need. Many people who cannot afford counseling could be helped into more productive lives. Everyone has identity issues because we live in a broken world that has impacted all of us. The potential benefits to reaching larger numbers of people in our communities with recovery resources are vast. If successful recovery programs expanded to the masses, community and family relationships would improve, work productivity would improve, and we would have more sustainable communities as a result.

Unsustainable Patterns of Community Living

Especially in recent decades, Western cultures have lived for individualistic cultural standards instead of the common good. However, systems set up to force the common good on nations have been the worst failures of all. It is only in democratic societies that a sustainable opportunity for the common good occurs. Unfortunately, we haven't been serving our neighbors in a way that takes the whole community into account. There is no clear cultural standard for outreach since the current cultural standard for success is that providing well for one's own family is enough.

Application to community service Most people feel overcommitted with family alone. Adding more to their schedule would be too much of a sacrifice, but prioritizing community service is more about valuing the right things and making the right kind of sacrifice. It's better for the families and communities to make time and give resources for community service than to sacrifice time and resources for expensive clothes or cars. When parents sacrifice to give their children expensive material items to meet the demands of their children, it usually has a negative impact on the child. Community service helps families value the right things. The service experience changes the people involved. I have seen the effect of community service on the people I have volunteered with.

Why cultural standards are not enough The cultural standard of only providing for one's own family is not sufficient to build sustainable communities. There will always be a small segment of society unable to care for themselves including those with physical disability and severe mental illness. Elitist societies do not make sufficient effort to care for the vulnerable. If the vulnerable are not cared for, elitist societies become even less compassionate. It is a cycle that perpetuates itself. Over 200,000 mentally and physically disabled people were killed by the Nazis in World War II, one of the most elitist and least compassionate societies in history (see "Nazi," 2014).

Provision for one's own family has never been enough even for the well-provisioned family. Families need to be involved in outreach in order to become less individualistic. Helping the needy gives families a perspective of giving unconditionally which inevitably enhances relationships within the family. Helping others also provides an opportunity for children to understand the lives of those with few resources. Strong families are needed for strong communities. A dearth of community service and too much individualism weakens families because of the negative effects of selfishness on relationships. Weakened families lead to weakened communities and weakened communities lead to a weakened nation. Prosperous nations have cycled historically from prosperity to individualism and immorality, cultural decline, unsustainable governmental practices, national collapse, and sometimes war. The Roman Empire fell from within in this way (Dods, M., *City of God*).

In some important ways, people took better care of each other before government welfare programs became extensive. Entitlements without accountability and without healthy relationships tend to increase selfishness and isolation. These two elements have contributed to the rise in violent crime in American cities over the decades.

Isolation from healthy family and friends wears on people because it generates a mindset that no one cares followed by a sense that one has nothing to lose. I was isolated for many years, and I grew angrier as time passed, eventually controlling rejection by pushing others away in a rage. Entitlements create a cultural environment in which we no longer need to depend on each other because we expect or demand that the government take care of our needs. Such demands are to our own detriment.

There are legitimate reasons why people tend to not look beyond provision for their own family. If their resources are limited, they think that they don't have enough to offer to others. However, volunteering requires minimal financial resources and the return in personal growth is great. Uninvolved families don't realize how much community involvement would benefit their family because cultural standards tend to give us a false sense of accomplishment. However, success in the family while the community decays is not success in God's eyes. God condemned Israel's leaders who probably provided well for their own families but exploited vulnerable people for their own gain (Ezekiel 34).

Living for retirement   The cultural standard of retirement dominated by individualistic pleasure travel and other forms of enjoyment is a hoarding perspective because time and resources are not generously given back to the community. It is as if there is no debt to society. We don't deserve to keep everything for ourselves because all of us had the help of a variety of community resources to establish our lives — resources such as the educational system, government services, news and educational media services, and a network of mentors from each phase of life (Gladwell, M., *Outliers*). Retirement years have maximum impact if applied for the common good.

The retirement generation is the only generation that has the opportunity to pass along life lessons to the next generation. They are often the only generation with sufficient experience and maturity to navigate people through the roughest relationship waters and the biggest problems. If the climax generation doesn't give back, then the younger generation is missing out on all those lessons. If the younger generation doesn't listen, that is not the responsibility of the older generation. However, more of the younger generation would listen and learn if given the opportunity.

Living for individualistic success   Large amounts of resources aren't getting passed to the next generation. Many with excess resources have no desire to pass it along. They're content to spend their resources on themselves thinking they owe nothing back. Climax generation members with a large excess in resources have the opportunity to direct exactly where they want their resources to be applied for maximum impact in the community. It's an once-in-a-lifetime opportunity. The richest country can take care of its own people and still help other nations. According to a study published by Oxfam, "The world's 85 richest people own as much as the poorest 50% of humanity" (Neuman, S., 2014). Too many give too little perhaps because they think they did it all themselves.

Living off the government   Decades of failed low-income housing projects in every major city brought awareness of the futility of giving people resources without accountability. It created an entitlement culture among the poor. The results were unsustainable and housing projects such as Cabrini-Green in Chicago came down. "During the worst years of Cabrini-Green's miseries, residents endured rat and cockroach infestations, rotting garbage in trash

---

61

chutes, the stench of urine and insecticide in hallways, malfunctioning elevators, graffiti on walls, as well as problems with basic utilities, such as bursting pipes" (see "Cabrini," 2014). Entitlement programs without mentoring or accountability have never worked. They are an extreme to be discarded.

The Extremes   In summary, sustainable communities must minimizing extreme patterns by addressing the extremes of insufficient giving and entitlement abuses in housing, healthcare, and food. Some people take food stamps that they don't need. Some people take farm subsidies that they don't need. Some oil companies with vast profits take subsidies that they don't need. If we cut out the waste of the extremes, we would be on the way to a surplus. The failure to ask for any sort of sacrifice from the general population and the failure to eliminate obvious waste are extremes in themselves, and it reflects the absence of effective leadership in all levels of government.

Sustainable Patterns

Ask everyone to give back   A large number of people with skills and resources do not give anything back to the community. Even moderate, non-sacrificial giving of time, talent, and resources would make a huge difference. To make matters worse, many of those that give nothing back demand more for themselves.

People without significant financial resources can still make a big difference through volunteering their time, experience, and skills. Entitlement programs have proven that receiving assistance without giving back doesn't work. It is important for the well-being of aid recipients to be involved in helping programs that helped them, because giving back negates entitlement thinking. Entitlement thinking is unsustainable because it ensnares people into a dependence on externals and keeps them from doing what they can. Giving back breaks the entitlement dependencies. Making sustainable sacrifices for the common good helps those who give and the aid recipients. Therefore, we should ask everyone to give back. The younger generation can give back by supplying the majority of volunteers. Volunteering is one the best ways this generation can find their niche in life and the community. They have abundant energy which is a great resource. The young generation should specialize in volunteering because they are learning the ropes and have the energy to spend.

Passing on life lessons Passing along life lessons is perhaps the greatest opportunity in life. Retirement age is when we pass along all that we've learned to the next generation. It's potentially the most productive time of life because members of the climax generation have learned to maximize efficiency and impact. John Maxwell is the best example. He's taking full advantage of a lifetime of lessons to pass along to the next generation through his books, personal growth plans, and mentoring programs (Maxwell, J., 2014), and he's doing it at maximum efficiency. For those in retirement who don't know how to pass along their life lessons, John Maxwell's resources can help them do exactly that. We would have stronger communities if there were more like him passing along life lessons to the next generation. He also has a plan to progressively distribute his resources for lasting impact in the community. Many communities would benefit if others followed his example.

Lesson transference increases sustainability because it negates the inefficiency of each new generation

---

reinventing the wheel of life lessons. It saves time, money, and energy for individuals and businesses. It also helps the trainer generation maintain their own skills. Whatever we don't use, we lose. Giving back always helps both sides.

Passing along resources   The untapped resources from wealthy individuals is a large potential difference maker. Some, like Bill Gates and Warren Buffett, recognize the help they had along the way and are giving back generously and making a huge impact (Gladwell, M., *Outliers*). They are the best examples for several reasons. They are among the richest and give the most away. They have the most reasons to believe that they did it themselves and yet they don't. They could have stopped working long ago and yet they are maximizing their impact in the world. The Bill and Melinda Gates Foundation is making a global difference in vaccine development and distribution, education, and agricultural development (Mundel, T. et al., 2014). In addition, Bill Gates has funded innovative companies like TerraPower, which has the potential to address nuclear waste issues and generate safe and reliable energy (see "Ideas," 2014). Bill Gates is maximizing his impact. If all retirement age people were actively passing on their resources, their knowledge, and their skills, there would be immediate and substantial results in all areas of need.

Accountable community regardless of viewpoint   A sustainable community gets the obvious done no matter the diversity of viewpoints. A sustainable community is able to work together and maintain long-term sustainability in its finances, families, waste handling, water supplies, and air quality. It is because people haven't taken up their unique niche in the community that we have pollution, poverty, abortion, or any other obvious issue. We can start with one obvious issue and agree on the obvious. For example, we should be able to agree that the earth has limited resources and people have limited finances and stay within safe limits. Many books, including this one, recommend safe limits for personal, community, financial, and environmental sustainability. We need to recognize safe limits and live within them.

How to Transition from an Unsustainable Community to Sustainable Community

The civil rights movement was a non-violent, truth-in-love coalition and they changed culture. People and the laws changed at the state and federal levels, so the civil rights movement can be a model for a large-scale culture transformation. The civil rights movement did not eliminate racism but the changes that took place were massive. Before the movement, large segments of southern culture had extreme views of race and believed blacks to be inferior humans (Branch, T., *America in the King Years*). The proportion of people who would hold such a view today is very small. This provides hope for the scale of change possible for just causes.

The need and rationale for a sustainability movement is more compelling because it affects all races worldwide. There's no reason why the sustainability movement couldn't achieve or exceed the scale of the civil rights movement. The rationale is clear. Unsustainable patterns are combining to put large segments of the global population at risk and change needs to begin now if we are to avoid permanent damage to the resources we depend on for survival. There is no rational reason that people cannot learn to accept and promote safe limits for personal, financial, community, and environmental sustainability. It must start on the local level before expanding to the state and federal levels. Unsustainable communities can become sustainable by loving our neighbor, serving our neighbor, and holding each other accountable. A short-term example is offering to take our neighbor's recyclables to the recycler and asking them to join us. A long-term example is families adopting families. This is a multifaceted process that involves giving of time, resources, and mentoring from one family to another over several years (Keller, T., *Generous Justice*). World Relief's refugee resettlement program has helped resettle over 250,000 refugees in 35 years through local churches, community mentors, and families (see "Celebrating," 2014).

Sustainable change requires long-term commitments from both the mentor and the mentee because people change slowly. It takes a long time to unlearn old habits and learn new habits. A holistic life-on-life approach is needed in order to address the whole person and identify root causes. As inspectors know, problems keep coming back if root causes are not addressed. Mechanical problems are easier to address than human problems. To address the root cause of a human problem, comprehensive, long-term, community-based personal mentoring is needed because people are complex and deep change usually comes only with high levels of effort. Personally, I began counseling almost 15 years ago. I plan to have mentors for the rest of my life. In addition to mentoring, there are common needs for healthcare, financial mentoring and assistance, job training, and basic material needs like food and clothing.

The Value of Sacrifice for the Community

I learned a difficult lesson about sacrifice through high school wrestling. As a freshman, it was enough for me to just go out for the team. However, I had the opportunity to wrestle varsity my first year if I dropped a weight class. I didn't make the sacrifice because the thought of getting embarrassed on the mat was too much. The opportunity to wrestle varsity came again my sophomore and junior years if I cut weight, but I rationalized that cutting weight would adversely affect academics, my first priority. I didn't understand or value that this was a sustainable sacrificial well worth the cost. I used academics as an excuse, and I knew something was wrong. I chose to wrestle off with a senior varsity co-captain my junior year and lost. I didn't plan to go out my senior year because I had burned out after so many missed opportunities. To everyone's complete surprise (especially mine), the seniors elected me a co-captain for my final season, probably because the senior captain who knocked me out of varsity competition felt bad about my loss.

What ensued my senior season was unforgettable. At that point, I had wrestled only a couple of varsity matches in my three years of wrestling. A wrestler with an excellent varsity record dropped a weight class and knocked me out of competition. I spent the entire season as a co-captain on the bench. The experience was so painful that I suppressed it for years. I couldn't talk about it until recently because I had never grieved the loss. It remained frozen.

While I was driving to my hometown Christmas Eve 2013, it dawned on me what I had missed in wrestling: the value of sacrifice. I had not made the sacrifices necessary to lead the team well and prepare them for competition. I was given an honor I didn't deserve. Sacrifice was needed to lead the team well and there was no doubt that it would have been worth it.

Sacrificial giving results in better families, better communities, and more sustainable and responsible government. People are designed to serve one another and to be fully satisfied only when we have done the work

---

(Proverbs 13:4). Sacrificial giving must be balanced so that we do not burn out. A sustainable sacrifice is characterized by daily disciplines and thanksgiving. Planned daily activity with a positive attitude correctly manages the expenditure of energy. The New Testament describe sacrifices of praise (Hebrews 13:15; Romans 12:1) which are empowered by the Holy Spirit. An unsustainable sacrifice is based on selfish ambition and leads to burn-out of some type. Excess energy is expended without sufficient recharge due to the fear and resentment that inevitably accompanies selfish ambition.

Many factors can keep us from sacrifice. Fear of burnout can keep us from attempting something with burn-out potential. Burn-out is serious physiological business for those who have been through it. It is not something people want to experience more than once. The antidote to burn-out is a daily disciplines approach because daily consistency is much more sustainable than high ambition energy expenditures. Daily disciplines are long-term and are sustained by long-term motives. For example, William Wilberforce led the British anti-slavery movement. The movement took his entire adult life to complete. It took 18 years for the slave trade to end. He introduced bills year after year and experienced several brutal near-miss defeats along the way that would have ended efforts driven by selfish motives. He made daily sacrifices characterized by prayer and thanksgiving because he had a vibrant personal relationship with God and he knew that God had called him to the abolitionist cause (Metaxas, E., *Amazing Grace*). Slavery was abolished completely only a few days before he died. He received the news on his last day of consciousness (Metaxas, E., *Seven Men*).

Sacrificial action reinforces endurance and vice versa. Selfish motives are insufficient for the long-term because the wrong motives ensure burn-out unless personal change takes place. Rock bands driven by selfish ambition tend to burn out relationally and break up. High pressure careers in finance and law driven by selfish ambition tend to burn out. Money, recognition, and sex are insufficient to drive the perseverance needed for long-term battles. Abraham Lincoln lost many elections including two crushing defeats in the Illinois Senate race on his way to the presidency. After winning the presidential election, he chose his cabinet on the basis of their ability to help the cause of winning the Civil War. Salmon Chase, Lincoln's treasury secretary, was a good administrator, and he competently managed fundraising for the war effort. Chase was also a genuine supporter of abolition. However, Chase was obsessed with becoming president and he tried to subvert Lincoln's leadership and set himself up to win the next election. Lincoln was informed of many of the details of Chase's efforts to portray him as a poor leader. Chase also childishly submitted four resignation letters to Lincoln during this period even though Lincoln treated him well. Lincoln gave Chase important responsibilities in the drive to end slavery over loyal colleagues because Chase was a genuine abolitionist. Lincoln put up with very difficult people because he was driven by the causes of winning the Civil War and ending slavery. He was so focused on these efforts that he was mostly unphased by the details of Chase's many personal betrayals (Goodwin, D. K., *Team of Rivals*).

During his presidency, Lincoln realized that the survival of the nation was at stake. In the Gettysburg Address, he expressed the "resolve" in the cause that "this nation, under God, shall have a new birth of freedom, and that government of the people, by the people, for the people, shall not perish from the earth." Lincoln's example summarized how we can make sustainable sacrifices without burning out. Sustainable sacrifice is driven by a higher cause allowing one to endure personal suffering. The cause always involves serving others whether individuals, organizations, communities, or a nation. The cause is upheld by higher standards and empowered by a higher Authority. A higher purpose transcends feelings and limitations. Sustainability is a higher cause worthy of sacrifice because the survival of nations is at stake.

Jonah spoke of sustainable sacrifice in his calling to assist in the survival of the city of Nineveh. Jonah had separated himself from the close fellowship he had experienced with God by running from God's call. Jonah suffered high levels of pain during this separation, and he longed to be restored to intimacy with God (Jonah 2:1-7). When Jonah repented and came back into God's presence, he was very grateful and yielded to God's sacrificial call. "I with the voice of thanksgiving will sacrifice to You" (Jonah 2:9). Sacrifice for God accompanied by praise and thanksgiving is sustainable.

Characteristics of Every Sustainable Community

A diversity of viewpoints is common to every community, no matter the size, and those diverse viewpoints are what provide balanced, team-oriented solutions. Homogenous teams are limited by their lack of diversity. Communities are diverse teams and need everyone to perform their role. Communities have suffered because too many capable individuals are not involved in making a difference. Every community needs to take care of those who can't take care of themselves. There will always be a legitimate and significant segment of the population that is not able to care for themselves. I have a sibling in that category. There's more than enough resources to take care of the small portion of the population that genuinely can't take care of themselves. Every community needs to help those who can take care of themselves to do so. There are not enough resources to take care of those who can take care of themselves but choose dependency instead.

Perfect community We'll see what a perfect community looks like only in Heaven. Everyone will be performing their best-fit role at maximum efficiency. People with visions of Heaven in near death experiences forget earth during the vision because Heaven is so much better (Alexander, E., *Proof of Heaven*). If we do think about earth in Heaven, it is likely that we would wonder how we got anything done on earth.

Action Plans

Recovery
* Find a healthy, balanced community of friends in recovery like Celebrate Recovery.
* List your fears and resentments and ask a recovery friend to help you in the recovery journey. Everyone has a hurt, hangup, or habit.
* If you are not open to attending a recovery meeting, consider reading a recovery book such as *Life's Healing Choices* (Baker, J., 2007) or *Healing the Shame that Binds You* (Bradshaw, J., 2005).

How people with resources and skills can discover their community impact
* Read *Strengths Finder* (Rath, T., 2007) and find an opportunity in the community to apply your strengths.
* Determine the positive impact you would most like to make in the community and pick three or more organizations that could implement or facilitate your impact statement. Determine your cost of living and

your excess income (if any) and then maximize the difference you make in the community by giving to your target organizations or by investing in the community yourself.

Other ways people with resources can give back
- Mentor/adopt a family in need. It will help your family too.
- Mentor a top candidate in your circle of people and pass along your life lessons. There is an abundant supply of mentoring material available specific to your mentoring interests.
- Take unused clothes to the Salvation Army and/or food to your local food bank.
- If you are receiving unnecessary government entitlements or subsidies, consider terminating the assistance.

How people in need can give back
- If you have received assistance from an organization, volunteer your time to that organization or to the community.
- If you have recovered financially, give back to the organizations that helped you or to another community organization of your choice.
- If you no longer need entitlements, consider terminating the assistance.

How to build an accountable community
- Talk to your neighbor, build a relationship, ask how you can serve, and find out their interests and help them to serve.
- Talk to elected leaders. Communicate with your government leader or talk to someone who can and tell them what your community needs and what you're

doing in the community. Switch the discussion from entitlement to working together to address community needs.

Encourage elected leaders:
- to address tax loopholes and wasteful subsidies to large, profitable companies. Corporate income tax was only 10% of federal tax revenue for 2013 (See "Where," 2014).
- to address unsustainable government pensions.
- to address entitlement waste. Social programs accounted for about 60% of federal expenditures in 2013 (See "Where," 2014).

Chapter 3

Financial Sustainability

What is Financial Sustainability?

Personal sustainability has a significant effect on financial sustainability. Many professional athletes have gone bankrupt after earning millions because of the lack of personal sustainability. According to *Sports Illustrated*, 78% of former NFL players have gone bankrupt or are under financial stress because of joblessness or divorce two years after retirement and 60% of NBA players are out of money within five years of retirement (Wiles, 2012).

Financial sustainability is living within responsible spending limits based on income and assets. It is not the lack of debt that establishes financial sustainability. Most people need loans to purchase homes or other long-term investments. A loan is sustainable as long as the loan applicant does not borrow more than their income or assets can handle. A holistic definition of financial sustainability includes living within responsible spending limits in a way that sustains physical health, mental health, relational health, and community health.

Tipping Points or Resource Reservoirs

The following statistics indicate the widespread and increasing levels of unsustainable personal living and its effect on national finances. Dependency on social programs is one of the clearest indicators of the scale of unsustainable personal living and subsequently its impact on communities and the nation. Consider the following statistics on the federal budget:

2013 federal expenditures of tax dollars (see "Where" 2014):
- Social Security: 24%
- Medicare, Medicaid, and Children's Health Insurance Program: 22%
- Safety net programs: 12% (Pell grants, Supplemental Nutritional Assistance Program, Head Start)
- Total cost of social programs: 58%

Other federal expenditures:
- Defense and international security: 19%
- Interest on the debt: 6%
- Other programs: 18%
- about 4% on Research and Development (Hourihan, 2014)

Personal Sustainability Issues that Affect National Finances

Fifty-eight percent of tax dollars are being spent on social programs. Too much of this money treats the symptoms of unsustainable personal living instead of addressing the root cause. A better way to invest tax dollars would be to direct it toward sustainable personal and community change through research and development. If the majority of the budget was solution-directed instead of symptom-directed, our communities would be much healthier and people would be living more sustainable lives.

Obesity One of the most widespread and highest-impact areas of personal sustainability is obesity. About two-thirds of America's population is overweight, but the trend is toward two-thirds obese in the coming decades (Taubes, 2013). If money were proactively invested in preventative healthcare such as workplace incentives and infrastructure for exercise, weight loss, and good nutrition, the potential savings in future symptom-based expenditure is enormous. The root cause of obesity is food addiction based on a broken identity. However, it is a socially acceptable addiction so there is much resistance to identifying it as such. The obesity statistics indicate that food addiction is one of the most common addictions in America. Social acceptance facilitates denial, and the resulting costs of this large scale denial of both addiction and social responsibility by the masses have national financial impact as summarized by type 2 diabetes statistics from the CDC listed below and the following statistic. Forty-eight million people, 15% of our population, are in the SNAP program (formerly food stamp program) and many of these individuals are obese (McMillan, T., 2014). This is a financial issue that the public can address, so it is explored in more detail in Chapter 6.

Factors that lead to poor nutrition in low income families include the types of food available at food banks, the lack of nutritional knowledge, and the lack of communities that promote nutrition. Processed foods are prominent at food banks because they contain subsidized ingredients that reduce their cost. Unfortunately, many of these foods are high in sugar and low in nutrients. People with good intentions transfer food from bakeries to food banks in order to avoid food waste and to provide food to needy families. However, high sugar, low nutrient foods do more harm than good. The top sources of calories for low income individuals were as follows (McMillan, T. 2014):

1. soda, energy drinks, and sports drinks
2. chicken dishes
3. grain-based desserts
4. yeast breads

5. tortillas, burritos and tacos
6. pizza
7. next category (beef dishes) was way down the list

America's obesity and porn issues are examples of the difficult nature of change and how things that are slow to change affect us financially. Change is difficult due to the resistance to addressing root causes instead of symptoms. It is useful to examine the potential reservoirs for change. Modern welfare programs did not begin until 1935 with the Social Security Act (see "US Welfare," 2014). More recently, federal welfare programs expanded almost four-fold since 1965 (Tanner, 2012). The potential alternative is obvious: if people helped each other within communities and replaced the welfare expansion, the potential effect is reduction of current welfare spending to one-fourth of its current cost. Before current programs became predominant, there was less crime and people took more responsibility for helping others. People helping people within communities is a much more sustainable path. Government programs have given the general sense that we don't need to take responsibility for our communities. There is no theoretical limit to the amount that welfare can be reduced by the outreach of fellow members of the community–as long as the majority of the population lives sustainably.

Where the masses tip When averaged out over a large population, if more than half of the population on average does not make a financial contribution to the local and national communities, the scales will probably begin to tip toward unsustainability. Forty-three percent of American households paid no income tax (see "Where," 2014), but almost everyone pays taxes of some kind. Many of those paying no income tax still contribute payroll taxes. The main issues are closing tax loopholes, cutting waste, and establishing reasonable tax rates across all income levels above the poverty line.

The number of people unable to take care of themselves is relatively small. About 5-6% of the population is severely hindered by debilitating conditions outside their control, and about 20% have some type of disability (Brault, M., 2012). Almost 95% can take care of themselves at some level. Most of these people are able to help others at a significant level. We are a nation full of people who are capable of both sustaining themselves and helping others.

If intra- and inter-community assistance involving family-to-family and peer-to-peer interactions reduced the social program expenditures to low levels, we would potentially have almost half the federal budget to address our debt, develop new solutions, and develop new technology to deal with sustainability issues. Even if mass volunteerism was able to bring us back to pre-expansion levels of social program spending, our elected leaders could still find ways to spend the country into a crisis. Thus, citizens must begin holding the government accountable to spend responsibly.

Social program expenditures are an enormous potential buffer for handling financial and community sustainability issues. There are still enough people with excess resources to help those that cannot meet their own needs or are not living sustainably. Tax loopholes should be closed on individuals and corporations with abundant resources. Higher taxes did not hamper the economy during the 90s. It was one of the most prosperous periods in our history. The wealthiest people need to pay more in taxes and give more to the community, and those with below average resources should not pay too much or too little in taxes. It doesn't make sense for those below the poverty line to pay taxes, but they could volunteer in the community. Everyone should give back something to the community because it benefits both them and the community.

Balancing tax rates   Financial sustainability is probably the most practical reason people need to help people. Americans vote mainly for economic reasons. If we could see or experience the long-term national financial consequences of not helping people, most would probably increase their community involvement significantly simply for its practical significance to their own financial stability. Proportional taxes as mentioned in Chapter 2 may should have conditions on both ends. Options could be given to the taxpayer to pay taxes in the form of community investment. The government could recognize community agencies that contribute to community sustainability based on objective criteria and then recognize taxpayer contributions to projects that save the government money as tax. It would be a recognition of investment that the government no longer needs to make. Chances are very good that this kind of community investment would yield far better results than programs administered by the government. On the government end, agencies at the state and federal level that do not manage tax income well based on objective criteria should have restrictions on any additional funding or cuts in funding until the agency meets the criteria. Illinois, for example, has the worst record for financial management. Tax increases did not result in effective debt management because financial management fundamentals are in disarray (see "Illinois Drowning," 2014). Since pension funding makes the largest contribution to debt mismanagement, that revenue stream needs restrictions.

There are reasonable compromises that the masses can make to work toward long-term financial sustainability. The highest tax brackets during and after World War I ranged from 67-73% during 1917-1921. The all-time high tax rate for the wealthy was over 90% during World War II. From 1941-1963, the highest tax bracket ranged from 81-94% and it remained above 70% until 1980 (see "History," 2014). People were expected to sacrifice for the greater good and they did. If clear economic tipping points become apparent, it would not be unreasonable for people to adopt an attitude of sacrifice for the greater good to prevent a crisis that would affect everyone. Everyone would make a contribution. Congress would be expected to manage the debt responsibly and make unpopular decisions to cut wasteful programs and increase taxes.

If reasonably higher taxes for a period of time would help prevent a crisis that could force businesses into bankruptcy, it's better for the wealthy to pay higher taxes. A 50% tax rate for the wealthiest Americans would be in line with historical norms, it would not significantly affect their lifestyle, and it would help to manage the debt much better (Reich, R., *Aftershock*). After World War I, a 50% tax rate was well below the average high tax rates until 1980. There is a range of reasonable tax rates for the wealthy. In 2011, the average tax rate was 20.9% for the top 5% of taxpayers (Pomerleau, K., 2013) – undoubtedly on the low end of 20th-century tax ranges. Likewise, 23.5% average tax rate for the top 1% of taxpayers in 2011 (Pomerleau, K., 2013) doesn't come close to top tax rates following World War I. Consistent, long-term management of the debt would negate the need for higher taxes. Apart from politics and personal wills, debt management for the U.S. would be possible because of the resources available in this country.

The counterpoint to higher tax rates for the wealthy is that they pay a disproportionate amount of the taxes. According to the Tax Foundation, the top 50% of all taxpayers paid 97% of all 2011 income taxes. The top 1% of all taxpayers paid 35% of all 2011 income taxes (Pomerleau, K., 2013). Therefore, a compromise taxation level is needed, not a historically high tax rate. It is better to give the wealthy control of where that money goes because they probably spend most of it better than the government would. Most wealthy business people became wealthy because they were good money managers.

Almost everyone pays taxes. According to the Brookings Institute Tax Policy Center, 84% pay either income tax or payroll tax. Of those not paying either income or payroll tax, 9.7% were elderly and earned too little income for taxation, and 3.4% had income of less than $20,000. The remaining 1.3% were miscellaneous including income earned and taxed abroad, interest income on tax-free municipal bonds, those with large medical bills, and those with large business losses (see "Who," 2014).

The average income tax rate for the top 1% of all taxpayers was about three times higher than the rate for taxpayers in the 25-50% group (Pomerleau, K. 2013). However, the effective tax rate including all types of taxes was approximately 17-22% for all taxpayers (Williams, R. 2008). The difference in effective tax rates between the wealthiest Americans and the poorest is well out of proportion to the income difference. For example, today's executives can earn over $1 billion in a single year through the stock market (Rushe, D. 2013). The income difference for such an executive would be 50,000-fold greater than someone earning $20,000 a year. Warren Buffet pointed this out himself in the "Buffet Rule" which states that the wealthy should not pay lower effective tax rates than middle class individuals. A secretary should not pay a higher effective tax rate than a CEO (Berkowitz, B. 2011). Closing tax loopholes around capital gains and dividends would vastly increase tax revenue. Current tax rates on capital gains and dividends allow some of the wealthiest people to legally reduce their effective tax rates to 15% (Berkowitz, B., 2011).

Effectiveness of people-to-people assistance and solution-oriented investment People-to-people assistance is not new. It was a mechanism for helping the needy before the massive expansion of government welfare programs. There is no theoretical reason why the number of people helping people cannot increase to replace much of the assistance offered by welfare. There are enough capable volunteers to assist those currently dependent on government resources. A healthy community can aid those dependent on government assistance and help them gain their independence. This is a natural choice to anyone who experiences the superior effectiveness of volunteer assistance. Volunteers provide an alternative to political approaches that haven't worked for decades. If volunteers do not rise to the challenge, the financial waste will continue and the U.S. economy will likely tip. It is better to implement steady change now than to tip later.

A volunteer approach works around politics. If communities working together fend people off government assistance in a healthy way, it eliminates the need for wasteful spending. The wasteful agencies would need to downsize or be eliminated. Positive results on a large scale could bring politics back into the picture as a viable option. However, it would only be to facilitate what worked and not to allow dependence on government assistance. The goal is to build stronger communities, not to increase the size of government. It is unlikely that wasteful healthcare and welfare spending will be significantly reduced unless the need for these services is reduced.

About 4% of the federal budget is spent on research and development (Hourihan, 2014). In a solution-oriented society, it is not unreasonable to consider the effect of a 10% investment of the federal budget in research and development (R&D). Funds for R&D can have an impact in any area, not just science and technology. For example, R&D funds could help us understand and create novel, diverse, and functional people-to-people assistance programs and non-profit-to-people assistance unique to the communities in which they are applied by collaborating with a combination of local and outside leadership.

This type of assistance is an example of how a well run government program can have a massive impact. The U.S. has had the best science overall for decades because of the combination of innovation-friendly factors that developed during and after World War II including our rigorous peer review system required for funding and publication. Most major research discoveries that modern technology is based upon were made in the U.S. All modern technology can be traced to some type of R&D funding. Why then, do we not increase funding for R&D and decrease it for programs that have not worked such as symptom-based social programs with the exception of those who are unable to care for themselves and who lack financial support from family. Otherwise, any competent organizational leader makes the obvious diversion of funds from unsuccessful programs to successful programs.

How Does Personal Sustainability Affect Financial Sustainability?

There are a few issues that affect all of us because they affect the financial health of the nation. As the figures listed above suggest, healthcare and social programs consume about 60% of the federal budget. Limited time and resources necessitate prioritizing the issues that have national impact.

Healthcare Without holistic personal sustainability, people do not take responsibility for their health, and this puts an unnecessary burden on community, state, and national finances. The obesity trends in the U.S. are one of the clearest examples of national financial impact. Obesity brings with it a wide variety of health issues including degraded cardiac health, decreased mobility, some cancers, and increased risk for type 2 diabetes (see "Obesity," 2014). Medical care for cardiac and diabetes patients can be very expensive. If the U.S. reaches an obesity level of 67% or more, it is unlikely that the health care system could fund or provide adequate care for this number of patients (Taubes, 2013). Consider the following 2014 summary statistics from the CDC and the financial impact personally and nationally (see "A Snapshot," 2014):

Eighty-six million (35%) currently have pre-diabetes and 90% of these individuals don't know they have pre-diabetes!

- 15-30% of prediabetics will develop type 2 diabetes within five years.
- 9% currently have diabetes
- Medical costs for people with diabetes are twice as high.
- People with diabetes are at higher risk for the following serious health complications.

- o Blindness
- o Kidney failure
- o Heart disease
- o Stroke
- o Amputation of toes, feet, or legs
- Risk of death for people with diabetes is 50% greater.
- The total cost of diabetes including medical costs, lost work and lost wages was $245 billion.

It is better to provide preventative healthcare incentives now than to deny care later due to insufficient resources. One of the strongest incentives for holistic personal sustainability is community. According to the *Daniel Plan* (Warren R. et al., 2013), a workout partner greatly increases the likelihood of maintaining an exercise and nutrition program. Currently, there are too many people that do not maintain their physical health in spite of being aware of the consequences. Many of these are very responsible and skilled people in all other aspects of life. Overeating is highly acceptable in our culture. Some restaurants compete for the biggest portion sizes. In Boston, the Eagle's Deli offers a burger containing five pounds of beef, 20 pieces of bacon, and 20 pieces of American cheese (Lew, 2010). Convenience stores are stocked with candy, snacks, and high sugar drinks. TV channels have outrageous eating contests. Joey Chestnut of San Jose, California, set the world record for eating 69 Nathan's Famous Hot Dogs and Buns in 10 minutes in 2013 (Shaw, 2013).

Financial incentives for exercise and nutrition can be estimated based on the cost savings in health expenditures. In his book *Fast Food Nation*, Eric Schlosser (2001) states that the annual health care costs in the United States stemming from obesity approaches $240 billion. As the CDC statistics indicate, the cost for obesity is far higher than this since the cost for diabetes alone is currently $245 billion. This is much more than the total federal expenditures on research and development. Based on this, a non-obese populous could easily double our current investment in research including significant investment in proactive approaches to sustainability issues. In other words, we could take significant steps toward financial sustainability simply by losing weight! Tax incentives for preventative healthcare are appropriate since taxpayers end up paying for medical costs of obese patients. Workplace incentives are appropriate because obesity affects workplace productivity and employer health insurance costs. It is likely that responsible people will respond well to attractive incentives such as discounts on their health insurance premiums. There should be penalties for those who continue unhealthy behavior in spite of repeat warnings from their doctor. Obesity-related health issues tend to accumulate over time, so an effective system would address obesity before the onset of a concentrated series of health problems.

The cost savings from preventative healthcare is attractive not only to the individual but also to communities, where cost savings can be invested. Based on health care costs in the federal budget, the size of investment in community improvements stemming from preventative healthcare savings is very large. Incentives are solution-oriented and long-term, and they can save providers the unpleasant task of denying healthcare in the future. National healthcare coverage is not a guarantee in a system that is overwhelmed by an unhealthy population.

Relational health I have struggled with an issue that will likely have national sustainability impact, pornography. For several reasons, porn affects personal sustainability

---

and, eventually, it may affect national sustainability. Porn creates problems relationally, mentally, physically, and, most of all, spiritually. These issues combine to create distance in relationships, break trust, and create unnecessary conflict. The scale of porn's impact is vastly expanded by the ease of private access on computers and mobile devices. About 90% of boys have viewed porn (see "Pornography," 2014).

The iPhone emerged in 2007, and smart phones have become predominant in the years since. Ease of private access to porn on mobile devices is still a recent phenomenon. Porn alone may or may not be sufficient to have a significant impact on personal and financial sustainability, but the combination of porn with the expansion of online dating services can potentially have devastating consequences for marriage, the basic unit of community. Without an appreciation for the value of the marriage covenant, the barriers against finding a new mate have been substantially reduced. In addition, the legal barriers to divorce have been reduced. Because financial hardship is closely linked with divorce, widespread financial impact of porn will likely come through divorce.

Spiritual health Spiritual health impacts financial sustainability in terms of how much we save, how much we give, what we give to, and whether we hold our elected leaders accountable for taxpayer dollars. Spiritual wellbeing has a positive impact on spending and giving. People who are spiritually satisfied tend to spend less on themselves and give more away. For example, Rick Warren, author of *The Purpose Driven Life* (2012), gives away over 90% of his income, as did equipment manufacturing entrepreneur R.G. LeTourneau (LeTourneau, R. G., *Mover of Men and Mountains*). Spiritual health affects finances universally because it is at the root of financial sustainability.

Why Giving is Part of Financial Sustainability

Hoarding is not personally sustainable because of the effects of greed on our relationships with God and others. Greed promotes a high level of selfishness and a low level of giving both materially and relationally. According to Luke 12:13-21, greed corrupts the hoarder. It leads to associating material gain with success, purpose, and keeping score in relationships.

Material generosity and relational generosity do not have a direct correlation, but one can facilitate the other. I enjoy giving to charities and have consistently given away a significant percent of my income since college, but I have not often been generous with forgiveness. Conversely, there are people who are generous with forgiveness but not with their money. Whatever form of generosity a person possesses can be a facilitator to improve areas where they need growth. Eventually, the strong areas can help raise the weak areas to an acceptable level. I've noticed that when I am serving in a food bank or homeless ministry, I have less resentment because volunteering influences my view of others in a positive way. A friend once recommended that I intentionally participate in community service with someone I had much resentment toward. Serving together didn't fix our broken relationship, but it helped. Later, another friend recommended that I keep forgiving until the resentment stopped coming up. That made a huge difference. I got together with the person I had resented so strongly "one more time" and the resentment lifted. I had not wanted to get together, but I ended up enjoying our time together, and the resentment hasn't come back since that meeting. Resentment can return any time I begin to keep score, but, after experiencing the relief of forgiveness, keeping score doesn't make much sense.

If a forgiving person is not generous materially, it may eventually affect their relational generosity. This is why it is important for everyone to establish a consistent pattern of material generosity. Failure to maintain one area in life affects other areas. Material generosity is important for maintaining relationships in the long-term. Our sphere of relationships, in turn, affects a wider network of people in the community. The people we know are in touch with people we don't know. Material generosity is particularly important for this wider community network. If we initiate with material generosity to our neighbors in need, it builds community relationships. Voluntary redistribution of our excess speaks clearly to those in need, but even more so does its absence. Community relationships can be some of the most rewarding and most surprising relationships. They involve giving time and resources to help get lives back on track and to break down cycles of hopelessness in both the recipient and the giver. For example, visiting with clients at a homeless shelter was the highlight of my week during my worst crisis period, and it was the only activity that significantly countered my hopelessness.

John Perkins is a minister, civil rights activist, and community developer who seeks to restore under-resourced communities. His ministries are good examples of intentionally building multiethnic and interracial leadership for community development using a combination of outsiders and people within a struggling community (Keller, T., *Generous Justice*,). He and his family spent 35 years helping struggling communities in Mississippi and California. He initiated with other leaders to establish the Christian Community Development Association (CCDA) in 1989 which uses relocation, redistribution, and reconciliation to assist disadvantaged communities (see "About," 2014). CCDA helps facilitate the movement of caring, well-resourced individuals into struggling neighborhoods to help revitalize the community and build businesses.

Financial Accountability through Community Investment

Accountable communities spend and invest wisely. Wise community investment is not difficult; there is a healthy diversity of reputable community service organizations already in place. Each person can pick a set of reputable organizations in their target areas and start investing their time and resources. People may also have a desire to meet specific community needs by starting new organizations.

Healthy people not only invest in the community, they hold leaders accountable for proper management of tax revenue for long-term sustainability. There are a variety of ways to do this. Direct interaction is not a practical or effective means of accountability in most cases. Perhaps the best means of holding government accountable for wise management of financial resources is to invest wisely as individuals and organizations in the community. Investment of time and resources directly in the community is far more effective than political methods. Most people don't argue with results. Even if our leaders are not spending tax revenue wisely, individual investment by the masses can begin to create financial sustainability by reducing the need for symptom-based healthcare and welfare programs. Programs like CCDA can have a major impact here. It is not necessary to have political power to create change.

Healthy people invest in the community by paying their taxes. In spite of wasteful government spending, there are still many vital government agencies from which we all benefit, including education, defense, agriculture, and science-based agencies. Too many people fail to recognize the contribution that government agencies have made to them. Insufficient tax revenue from individuals and corporations are contributing significantly to financial and community sustainability issues. Corporations contributed only 10% of the federal tax revenue in 2013 (see "Where," 2014) and only about 13% of their profits (Worstall, 2013). Highly profitable companies like Apple find ways to legally minimize their taxes. Although Apple paid full corporate taxes on U.S. profits, foreign profits can be taxed at much lower rates (Worstall, 2013). Companies should not pay taxes on income that is not made in the U.S. In spite of the relatively low overall contribution to federal tax revenue at a time of record profits, the U.S. has the highest combined corporate federal and state tax rates of all developed countries at 39%. Japan is next at 37% followed by France at 34.4%. Ireland has the lowest rate at 12.5% (Helman, 2014).

Although many corporations have been very generous to community development, the contribution of the most profitable companies is not in alignment with their profits. Exxon Mobil's 2012 profit was almost $45 billion. The lowest 2012 profit of the top 20 companies was almost nine billion dollars (Ziegler, T. et al., 2013). Total corporate income for 2010 was 1.4 trillion (Worstall, T., 2013). Highly profitable companies should not pay more taxes than the law requires, but they should invest in communities in proportion to their profits in order to maintain a healthy balance for the company and the community. Exxon Mobil donated 0.3% of 2011 pretax profits to charity in 2012, which was the lowest percent of the top 10 donating companies. The second lowest was another oil company, Chevron's 0.6% (Gose, B. et al., 2013). By this measure, oil companies are the greediest companies.

A culture of greed is harmful to companies. Companies that miss the necessity of putting checks and balances on themselves endanger their longevity. Cultural mishaps can doom companies, as seen in the Enron scandal. Giving generously is a culture protector for the company, and an investment in their own future. Greed may seem to be the quick path to financial security but, in reality, it is the fast track to financial unsustainability through cultural demise.

It is the company's responsibility to determine how they will spend their profits. However, companies are part of larger communities and nations. Influential companies have significant impact on communities and nations because they create markets for products and services that affect sustainability. Companies are likely to be the only option when it comes to establishing needed changes quickly. People react quickly to the marketplace, but people do not change quickly. Thus, attractive sustainable products are more likely to facilitate sustainability in a timely manner than personal and community change. Sustainability scientists do not believe that societal behavior changes will come quickly enough to avoid the effects of carrying capacity overshoot (Randers, J. 2052). Purchasing changes do have the potential to achieve fast change as demonstrated by the speed with which new technologies are accepted. However, there is no guarantee that companies will bring the right products to the marketplace in time. One example of a high priority sustainability product would be a value added cover crop that would inhibit soil erosion and provide income sufficient to ensure its widespread use. If large biotech companies do not develop this kind of resource, perhaps a small startup company will. Companies have responsibilities to the communities and countries in which they do business – including personal, community, and environmental sustainability.

In addition to being indebted to communities, companies have a debt to the environment. If a company consumes a non-renewable and gives nothing in return, environmental imbalance is created. Environmental imbalance created in part by oil companies is now beginning to have high impact on the global community. Our finely balanced climate begins to tip when it has been tweaked. Climate change has a significant impact on both financial and community sustainability as seen in the rise of extreme weather globally (see Chapter 5).

Fossil fuels are one of the clearest examples of products that do not take into account their true cost to the community. Oil companies have a responsibility to the global community to give back in proportion to what they are taking from the earth, and they have a responsibility to their employees to build a long-term business that does not rely on a non-renewable resource. If oil companies do not respond to sustainability issues and create their own renewable energy business model, consumers will eventually put them out of business by purchasing cost-effective renewables. Tesla is proving that many consumers will pay a premium for high quality electric vehicles. As well, they are preparing a competitively priced vehicle with a 200-mile range for launch in the near future (Bullis, K., 2014).

Financial accountability for wasteful subsidies and pensions
Unnecessary and wasteful subsidies and pensions place a significant burden on financial sustainability. Highly profitable oil companies received at least ten billion dollars in government subsidies in recent years (McKibben, B., 2012). It is unwise to subsidize highly profitable companies producing a product that we need to phase out.

Profitable farmers also receive subsidies. Annually, about nine billion dollars in crop insurance subsidies go overwhelmingly to the richest farmers and agribusinesses. The wealthiest farmers collected over $1 million per year in insurance subsidies while the lowest 80% averaged about $5000 each (Stewart, J., 2013). Likewise, there are people on welfare and food stamps that don't need them. For example, a man who won two million dollars in the Michigan lottery in 2011 continued to collect food stamps (Stewart, 2013). Poorly managed pension programs are also significant contributors to financial unsustainability. In Illinois, a highway maintenance worker can earn up to $148,000 per year with overtime. Early retirement at age 50 after 25 years on the job can pay $75,000 per year. Tens of thousands of state workers, over 75,000 in California alone, now receive special retirement benefits such as early retirement once reserved for those in dangerous jobs such as policemen and firefighters. Early retirement or enhanced pensions are now available for lottery agents, crime-lab technicians, livestock inspectors, foresters, and coroners. The enhanced job benefits do not match the job duties and are putting states into deep debt (Frank, T., 2011). We are growing the national debt by giving entitlements to a broad spectrum of people and by not taking responsibility for other types of spending waste and revenue loopholes. Most people are not holding their elected representatives or their neighbors accountable for keeping such wasteful spending under control.

Factors that Could Lead to Economic Tipping Points

The interaction of debt and economic growth   For decades, the growth of economies in developed nations have hidden the potential consequences of rising national debts. The debt surpassed the size of the entire U.S. economy in 2012 (Wolf, R., 2012). The record low debt to GDP ratio was 31.7% in 1974 at the end of the "Great Prosperity" period (see "United," 2014). Growth of our economy has enabled it to service the debt thus far. However, if the economy stagnates or shrinks and the debt grows, it can move toward a ratio where the debt is too large for the economy to service. The responsible way to handle the debt long-term is to shrink the debt according to the size of the economy and the availability of resources. Margin for emergencies should be built into such planning so that the debt is considerably smaller than the size of the economy. Individuals are not allowed to borrow more than they can pay back. The government should not be an exception.

The years 1998-2001 are the only time since 1970 in which the federal budget deficit has had a surplus (Patton, M., 2012). Economies are complex. Because a variety of factors contribute to economic stability, debt ratios from one country cannot predict the economic tipping point for a different country. However, no country can escape the basic principle that an economy cannot service a debt that has become much larger than the economy itself. If the debt increases to levels much larger than the size of the total economy, the interest on the debt becomes too high to manage. Many countries will be in danger of reaching unsustainable debt levels in the coming decades if current trends continue.

In 2011, Greece's total debt was 170% of GDP, and Italy's total debt was 127% of GDP in 2012 (Allen, 2013). These are examples of countries that experienced economic chaos under the burden of unsustainable debt. A major depression can last for a decade or more during which the economy shrinks. If the U.S. economy shrank for an extended period and the debt increased a trillion or more per year, then it could take less than 15 years to reach 200% debt/GDP depending on how much the economy shrank. It is difficult determine whether the U.S. economy would experience a tipping point on the way to 200% debt/GDP, but it is better not to find out. If we are to have a reasonable chance at sustainable national finances, our leaders need continuous public pressure to manage the debt and economy responsibly.

We cannot rely on economic growth to hold off a debt crisis if that growth depends on accessing the earth's limited natural resources because we are approaching the maximum sustainable land use. An economy based on fixed resources will be forced to shrink when those resources become limiting, and it would continue to shrink as those resources are used up. Alternatively, we can grow the economy in ways that don't use more resources (renewable energy, next generation nuclear, reuse, recycling) or shrink the debt by managing federal money responsibly. We can make money through saving energy by using LED lighting, passive solar designs, and better insulation strategies. Renewable energy can create jobs. According to a report in *Scientific American*, solar energy for the whole country would generate more jobs than the fossil fuel industry (Zweibel, K. et al., 2008). Conventional and novel recycling technologies, such as landfill recycling, can reuse and convert previously extracted resources. The physical resource tipping point is the ultimate economic and sustainability challenge. If we pass a physical resource tipping point that limits food and water, survival itself will be at stake.

Potential effect of climate change on economic tipping points
According to a study by Klaus Jacob, Columbia University, Lamont Doherty Earth Observatory, New York City (NYC) could face a five foot rise (+/- one foot) in sea level by 2100. He also has predicted that extreme storms (one-in-100-year storms) could hit NYC every other year by 2080. The 2013 storm surge level sufficient to cause widespread destructive flooding in NYC was eight feet, and the Hurricane Sandy storm surge was 11 feet (Fischetti, 2013). The cost of Hurricane Sandy was at least $65 Billion (Rice, 2013), second only to Hurricane Katrina. The year 2100 storm surge sufficient to cause widespread destructive flooding in NYC will only be three feet if the east coast sea level rises five feet. The current value of property at risk for flooding in NYC is $2 trillion (Fischetti, 2013). NYC flood damage costs alone would be economically unsustainable for the federal budget if the federal government covered the majority of these costs. The value of the at-risk property in NYC is approximately half the size of the annual U.S. budget. Federal payment for the losses and movement of all affected coastal residents would be financially unfeasible.

A citizen-driven effort could provide an alternative to government disaster relief. East coast residents can help themselves and each other. Movement of residents in the lowest, most vulnerable areas can take place on a voluntary basis. A slow move beginning now and proceeding over the coming years would be much more sustainable and safe than a rushed move as a result of extreme storms and/or economic crises. If it is not possible for some residents in these areas to move themselves, citizen-driven programs could be established to help disadvantaged residents move voluntarily. Incentives at local, state, and federal levels should encourage voluntary movement of residents from at risk areas.

How Can Communities Prepare for, or Prevent a Financial Tipping Point?

The best time to prepare for a crisis is before it happens, while we still can. Once a crisis begins, it's too late to prepare. We can't predict when an economic tipping may occur, but we can prepare or even prevent one. A financial tipping point may be the first sustainability area to be affected by cumulative effects of personal sustainability issues. If financial sustainability is to be a reality, a significant percentage of people must begin living sustainably now. We must first deal with areas of denial that inhibit or preclude financial sustainability.

By dealing with denial Denial that current trends left unaddressed will lead to a financial tipping point is a significant factor for large segments of the population. Political campaigns for decades have shielded people from the realities of choices and sacrifices that the masses must make to attain long-term financial sustainability. Neither of the major parties have taken responsibility for deficit spending and have left the issue in the hands of economic growth. Demagoguery facilitated by denial has been the driving force behind the failure to ask the public to make necessary sacrifices and the failure to reign in deficit spending.

Possible variations of denial include:
- "I don't have time to deal with anything other than my family." Family should be the top priority, but community outreach benefits the families who get involved in helping others. This not only negates the time conflict, but turns it into a valuable time investment.

- "Even if I did something, it would not make a difference." A country with the wealthiest people and companies can make a major impact and significantly reduce the risk of crisis over time in spite of the damage done thus far.

- "There is no spending problem." I have talked to someone on the far left who thought current spending trends can continue far into the future. The financial system would not handle a prolonged decrease in the size of the economy combined with trillion dollar deficit spending.

- "Someone else will deal with it." Neither our elected representatives nor a majority of citizens have dealt with long-term federal spending issues thus far.

- "Somehow, everything will be fine if current spending trends continue even though there may be a problem." Every economy has a tipping point. The U.S. will tip at some point if the debt continues to outsize the economy.

By preparing without panic Awareness and calmness are both needed to prepare for or prevent a crisis. The potential financial realities are very harsh, but an effective response must be calm, consistent, and responsible. Long-term realities should be the motivator for consistent action now. Sustainable preparation leads to sustainability itself through incremental planning that adjusts to current realities. Such incremental action leads to sustainable growth because sufficient investments are made to secure the results long-term. Sustainable growth then leads to community and national change. Volunteerism can grow to massive levels in the community in this fashion by following and scaling up the approach of leaders like John Perkins.

Harsh realities must be addressed without being harsh. Based on this, power struggles and political approaches are not viable options. By volunteering, giving to effective organizations, and reaching out to our neighbors, we can produce sustainable change without dangerous power struggles. If we take our chances with current financial trends by doing nothing or relying on politics, history may have to teach us a lesson.

What if a Tipping Point Occurs?

Impact of volunteers   Our elected leaders have continued in a pattern of failing to do what's best for the nation. Our leaders have made entitlement promises to the electorate for political gain rather than asking everyone to sacrifice for the common good. Most people probably would be willing to sacrifice for the common good if they were aware of the alternatives. Unfortunately, people are short-sighted. Most don't live for the long-term. If we become financially unsustainable as a nation, volunteers would likely be the best way to help get the nation back on a sustainable path. The U.S. has had a history of volunteerism during crises like World War II (WW2) and recent disaster cleanup efforts from Hurricanes Sandy and Katrina. Over one million volunteers helped in the Katrina relief effort (Lopez, 2008). People made sacrifices for the greater good during WW2 such as paying higher taxes, provision of salvage materials, gas rationing, speed limits, food conservation, and recycling (see "Rationing" 2014). Masses helping the masses has happened before and it's the most practical option when a crisis occurs. Volunteers innovate in a crisis and meet the need. If enough volunteers help those in need, the likelihood of undesirable political solutions to a crisis is reduced. It is difficult to argue with someone who volunteers to help someone in need because this type of action is apolitical. Serving others usually calms communities and silences agendas.

Volunteers are the best approach to the greatest areas of need. Massive volunteerism to reduce the need for welfare programs is probably more practical than political approaches to debt management. If people can't give money, they can give their time, experience, and relational care to others. There is always something to give. Every volunteer can share their life, their experience, and their interests with others. Volunteers are the best option for the toughest jobs, because others don't want to touch these areas. Volunteering is also a valuable gift to the recipient because recipients realize that their helpers didn't get paid.

How to Become Financially Sustainable as a Nation

Action Plan

Reduce the need for social programs and entitlements through volunteerism and giving

- Begin the journey toward personal sustainability by putting into practice the principles and action steps in *Purpose Driven Life* and *Daniel Plan*. *The Daniel Plan* describes a holistic personal health plan that includes faith, food, fitness, friends, and life focus.

- Everyone has skills, interests, and experiences that can help a person in need. Consider how you can best help others in need with your skill and interest sets and volunteer with a local organization or find and help a neighbor in need. Target an area of healthcare or welfare in this chapter. Historically, intra-community assistance has had better results, more accountability, and far less waste than government welfare programs.

- If you are a person in need of assistance, start working with a non-profit organization, community volunteers, or a church in order to become more sustainable.

- If you have been a person in need and have become personally and financially sustainable, consider terminating government assistance. You can make a contribution to long-term sustainability by doing so.

- If you are able to pay taxes and able to give to charitable organizations and do not, consider the long-term financial and personal implications at the local and national levels of not giving back to the community.

- If you are already involved in volunteering and giving to charity, consider how you can help others become volunteers and givers or how you can expand your own service and giving. Consider working with existing organizations and programs in your community to help neighbors in need become personally and financially sustainable.

- If you attend a church, help your church become a difference-maker in the community.

- Send elected representatives results from volunteer activities.

Identify and cut waste

- If you are a profitable farmer or businessman accepting government subsidies, consider ending the assistance.

- If you are a government worker receiving early or enhanced retirement, consider the impact of your pension on financial sustainability. Can you contribute to reducing the government debt burden by helping a person in need or going back to work?

- If you are an executive receiving excessive compensation and paying low taxes, consider the impact your excess resources can have in the community and invest in an area of interest. Also consider modification of your company's executive compensation policies. Consider the impact your company's profits can make in the community. You can work with existing organizations to make an immediate and significant difference in the community.

- If you are an elected representative, consider introducing incentives to promote community service through charities and non-profits. Consider better accountability measures for entitlement programs and budget management. Consider strong incentives to businesses and individuals for preventative healthcare.

Chapter 4

Environmental Sustainability

Environmental Sustainability

What is environmental sustainability? The long-term capacity of ecosystems to support life without net losses of any type that would endanger ability of the ecosystems to support, repair, and replenish themselves.

Environmental sustainability is secondary in nature
Environmental sustainability has always been dependent on personal and community sustainability. It is secondary as a cause, but it is primary as an effect. It is the most irreversible of all sustainability types. Even though it is the most important symptom, it is not the most important area of sustainability since it is not the root cause. As in healthcare, treating root causes is always more important than treating symptoms. For example, if we fail to address the root cause of obesity, we will continue to treat symptoms like type 2 diabetes indefinitely. People don't lose weight with a symptom-based approach, and we may become financially unsustainable as a nation if we don't address root causes in healthcare. If people want to change, they will treat the root cause within themselves. This is more than an analogy. When people don't learn to live sustainably at the personal level, global sustainability is at risk.

We will not fix the environment by treating symptoms like cleaning up oil spills and reintroducing endangered species. These are important to do but they do not address root causes. The secondary nature of environmental sustainability was difficult for me to accept because I value nature for its own sake. I have spent years hiking alone in national parks, wildlife refuges, and other natural areas, and loving every minute of it.

Why environmental unsustainability is the most irreversible of all sustainability types The good news about personal, community and financial sustainability is that we can do something to correct trends in these areas. However, if non-renewable resources supplied by our environment are depleted, there is little or nothing we can do to replenish them depending on the resource. The soil is perhaps the most important example. It takes hundreds of years to build an inch of lost topsoil assuming that stewardship of the land allows for a net soil gain (Singh, A. 2005). However, most cropland is not managed for a new soil gain. Another conditional non-renewable resource is clean water. Resources to clean and distribute the water determine whether people can obtain adequate potable water.

Replenishment times vary depending on the resource. Soil replenishment takes hundreds of years, and fossil fuels take millions of years to form. Natural resources do not replenish overnight. The time required for nature to replenish resources is well beyond human life spans. Humans must manage resources so that they do not endanger their ability to provide for their own basic life needs.

Root Causes of Environmental Sustainability Issues

Individual There is great pressure in every culture to live up to cultural standards. For most of human history, the pressure has been directed toward obtaining trophy jobs and trophy spouses. People are driven to consume more than the sustainable level in order to meet cultural standards of success. Too many of the executives and managers of oil companies, mining companies, logging companies, chemical companies, and energy suppliers have become rich at the expense of the environment.

Corporate   Companies rarely consider the lifecycle or the environmental cost of their products, and governments have not held them accountable. The true cost of products is determined by more than the cost of the raw materials. It includes the cost to the environment of using the product and the long-term cost of disposal because, ultimately, air, soil, and water quality strongly affect our health and our ability to do business. It has been the norm to focus on profits at the expense of the environment. Hazardous chemicals and other forms of waste were routinely dumped untreated into rivers and the Great Lakes before environmental laws were passed. Environmental cost was a non-factor. This does not make sense for businesses because mistreating the environment increases the cost of doing business long-term. For example, as the easily-reached oil is depleted, new and more expensive drilling techniques are needed to obtain hard-to-reach reserves or lower quality fossil fuels are used (Biello, D. 2013).

It is not wrong to make a profit. However, companies that damage long-term environmental sustainability should work toward creating a sustainable business. Oil companies have enormous resources for creating new business and technology. They can invest those cash reserves in renewable energy for the greater good and secure their own business future by developing renewable energy technology potentially faster than anyone else. Unfortunately, they are wasting the opportunity that their cash reserves present. Oil companies and individuals have the same root cause issue, a broken identity that makes them dependent on cultural standards.

Unsustainable Environmental Practices

Increasing fossil fuel consumption   Fossil fuels are becoming harder to reach and lower in quality. Lower quality fossil fuels, such as tar sands, produce higher levels of emissions at a time when dramatically lower levels are needed. Large countries such as China and India are consuming more fossil fuels as they modernize and expand their economies. Climate scientists estimate that a 2 °C increase in the earth's temperature would bring about changes that would "harm all sectors of civilization" and that the maximum atmospheric carbon dioxide concentration to stay below a 2 °C increase is about 405 ppm (Mann, M., 2014). CO_2 levels briefly reached 400 ppm in 2013 for the first time in history. In order to limit CO_2 levels below 450 ppm, carbon emissions could rise only a few more years and then would have to decrease several percent per year. CO_2 levels interact with the climate's sensitivity to greenhouse gases to determine how fast the global temperature rises. If the climate has intermediate sensitivities, the 2 °C threshold could be reached between 2036 and 2046, beginning only 22 years from now (Mann, 2014). Unfortunately, greenhouse emissions are rising faster than ever (see "Climate," 2014) almost ensuring that the 2 °C threshold will be reached if current trends are not addressed.

Fracking   Fracking is a highly questionable technique used to obtain a relatively clean fossil fuel. It works by drilling vertically and horizontally followed by blasting in chemically treated water and sand at high pressure to fracture rock and liberate natural gas. A single horizontal bore requires 2-4 million gallons of water and 15,000-60,000 gallons of chemicals. There are several bores per site and each horizontal bore may be fracked multiple times. A significant 75% of the chemically treated water blasted down comes back up. Poor sealing of the bore holes and infiltration from waste water ponds are possible contaminants of river basins. Methane contamination was found in 51/60 private drinking wells in the Marcellus Shale region of Northeastern Pennsylvania and upstate New York. Wells closer to the drilling site had much more methane than those further away (Mooney, C., 2011). The technique largely negates the quality of the product obtained because it endangers a more valuable resource, freshwater resources. Once again, companies have rushed to make money without fully understanding the cost to the environment or to the local residents.

Tar sands   The energy required to refine fossil fuel's raw materials into final product continues to increase as the easy-to-reach crude oil is depleted and oil companies turn to other sources. This is measured by EROI, the energy harvested per unit of energy spent to obtain it. Tar sands have one-third the EROI of conventional oil. Production of tar sands has tripled over the past decade (Inman, M., 2013). Underground tar sands are more extensive than those on the surface and are becoming the primary raw material. Unfortunately, underground tar sands produce 2.5-fold more greenhouse gas emissions than surface mining. If we processed and burned all of Alberta's tar sands, they would contribute half of the global temperature increase thus far in history. The global carbon budget to stay within the 2º C threshold requires that less than half of the known, recoverable oil, gas, and coal reserves be produced. The global carbon budget also requires that greenhouse emission be reduced 2.5% per year starting now. Instead, greenhouse emissions continue to increase (Biello, D., 2013).

Torrential rains   A trend in extreme rainfall exists in localized patterns throughout the world. Warmer air increases evaporation and holds more water (Vergano, 2013) and water-holding capacity is expected to increase roughly exponentially with temperature (Min, S. et al., 2011). Extreme precipitation has increased 74% in the last 60 years, (Vergano, D., 2013). Some of the highlights include the worst flooding in the history of Pakistan in 2010 (Guerin, O., 2011), and major flooding in Iowa since 1990 including 1990-1993, 1996, 1998, 1999, 2001, 2002, 2004, 2007-2011 (see "Iowa," 2014). A study of the autumn 2000 floods in England estimated that the increased in risk of flooding attributable to anthropogenic greenhouse gases was likely to be more than 90% (Pall, P. et al., 2011). Two day rain totals in the Nashville area in 2010 were greater than 19 inches in some areas according to the National Weather Service Forecast Office, Nashville, Tennessee.

Climate change   There have been at least five major ice ages in the earth's history. Outside of these periods, it appears that the earth was ice-free (Warren, J., 2006). Climate change is part of earth's history, and it appears that humans are contributing to climate history. Of the top ten hottest years on record, nine were recorded after the year 2000. Since 1976, every year has been warmer than the long-term average (see "Climate," NASA, 2014). If the polar ice melts again, millions of people would need to move, since half of the world's population lives near the ocean coastlines. The total potential sea level rise from melting of all glaciers is 80.32m (Poore, R., 2000). Given the earth's geological history, we should expect climate change and plan accordingly.

Any significant sea level rise combined with a repeating pattern of extreme storms will require permanent evacuation of the affected coastal areas. If such movement is not well managed, there could be major impacts to arable land and the national debt. The number of people affected by a 1 m sea level rise was estimated to be 145 million (Anthoff, D. et al., 2006). The population affected by a 10 m sea level rise is estimated to be up to 10% of the world's population, currently around 700 million people (McGranahan, G. et al., 2007). A 10m rise in sea level would not be unexpected in the long-term given the vulnerability of the West Antarctic Ice Sheet. It is vulnerable because it is grounded below sea level (Poore, R., 2000). Millions of people moving inland would potentially take significant amounts of arable land out of crop production. The financial cost would be enormous. As mentioned in Chapter 3, the cost of vulnerable property in New York alone would be financially unfeasible.

Currently, no major governmental initiatives are addressing the need to move the most vulnerable residents now. The opposite is occurring. The incentives that encourage people to live in the most vulnerable areas are still in effect (Fischetti, M., 2013). The U.S. east coast is a hotspot for coastal flooding and erosion. The land along the east coast is sinking from the withdrawal of groundwater and melting arctic ice is changing Atlantic currents in a way that raises sea level along the coast. The result is the that east coast sea level rise is 3-4 times the rate as other coastal areas, an estimated total of 5-9 extra inches of sea level rise by 2100 compared to the average global increase (Fischetti, M., 2013).

Climate stabilization effects of the Amazon According to NASA, "The ability of these forests to hold onto carbon has beneficial implications for stabilizing the world's climate" (see "Landsat," 2012). As the world's largest rainforest, it is a major carbon sink. Proper management of the Amazon is an important target for both climate stabilization and biodiversity preservation. The Amazon Rainforest has a 25-fold greater carbon storage capacity than grassland (Goodland, R., and Anhang, J., 2009). Eighty percent of the Amazon remained as of 2012. Approximately 5% of the Amazon was lost between 2002 and 2012. More than 70% of Amazon forest cover may be necessary to maintain the forest-dependent rainfall regime (Soares-Filho, B., 2006). "About 50% of the rain that falls in the Amazon is generate by the forest itself" according to Stanford scientist Gregory Asner (Fraser, B., 2013). In the long-term, it is unlikely that the Brazilian government would be able to hold losses to 30% or less. If Amazon deforestation exceeding 30% in the 2030s results in further climate destabilization, the timing will coincide with the other critical sustainability factors such as population growth and land supply in the 2040s.

Areas of Highest Impact for Mitigating Climate Change

Diet change According to a study by Goodland and Anhang (2009), switching to non-red meat consumption may be the quickest and highest impact path to reducing greenhouse gasses (GHGs). A 25% decrease in livestock products worldwide by 2017 would result in a 12.5 % reduction in GHGs (Goodland and Anhang, p.15).

Livestock lifecycle and supply chain account for at least half of all GHGs (Goodland and Anhang, p. 11) including 37% of human-induced methane, which has a global warming potential 25-fold greater than carbon dioxide (Goodland and Anhang, p. 13). Other agricultural GHG estimates vary between 14-18% (Capper, J. et al., 2013). The Goodland study stated that other studies have greatly underestimated the contribution of agriculture to GHGs because of uncounted livestock respiration contributions, uncounted land use contributions, undercounted methane, and undercounting of livestock. Livestock production and supply chain uses about 26% of arable land worldwide to feed a total of about 50 billion livestock raised per year (Goodland and Anhang, p. 14). Thirty-three percent of arable land worldwide is used for growing feed for livestock (Matthews, C., 2006). A substantial increase in demand for livestock products from China and India is predicted to occur over the next 40 years (Capper, J. et al., 2013). Much of this growth is anticipated to be for beef production, the least efficient source of animal protein. According to *National Geographic's* comparison of animal protein sources, every 100 calories of grain produces 22 calories of eggs, 12 calories of chicken, 10 calories of pork, and 3 calories of beef (Foley, J., 2014). Increasing livestock and human populations compound the difficulty of reducing GHGs in the coming decades beyond the already difficult problem of facilitating diet behavior change in the current population.

Switching land use from livestock production to plant production would relieve significant burden from further Amazon deforestation since almost 90% of deforested land was converted to pasture (Kaimowitz, D. et al., 2004). Converting rainforest to pasture is extremely poor land management because it simultaneously removes the world's largest forest carbon sink and the largest biodiversity area. The carbon sink is needed for climate stability and the biodiversity is needed as a gene pool for future problem solving.

It would seem straightforward to ask people to sacrifice beef in order to preserve the world's most important biodiversity area for the sake of current and future generations. Significant reduction of beef consumption while maintaining pork consumption would still have an impact since pork is about three times as efficient.

Substituting poultry for both beef and pork would have very significant impact since poultry is about four times more efficient than beef. Diet change does not require technological breakthroughs or infrastructure changes that may take decades as in the case of renewable energy. It can be implemented as soon as people decide to alter their diet. Yet, human behavior modification is one of the most difficult changes to facilitate.

Food Sustainability

We live on a finite planet with finite resources. Current levels of consumption are beyond what the earth can support in the long-term. We currently consume at the rate of about 1.5 Earths. (Randers, J., 2052). In other words, we are depleting our natural resources faster than they can be replaced by about 1.5 times. In considering likely future consumption rates, it is not unreasonable that consumption rates in 2050 would total to around three Earths. If consumption rates do not adjust, resources for basic living needs including food and water will become limited at some point. We are using up our reserves at an unsustainable pace. If food and water resources become limited on a global level, the level of conflict generated by entitlement living in that scenario would be unsustainable and perhaps unrecoverable. The stakes for the next three decades could not be higher for the world community.

Arable land supply and food sustainability The amount of available cropland per person is 0.27 hectares/ person. The minimum amount of cropland needed for feeding one person on a plant diet is about 0.2 hectares (Singh, A. *One Planet, Many People*, 2005). This minimum will be reached when the global population reaches around eight billion

(Singh, A., 2005, p. 27) in the early 2040s (Randers, J., *2052*, p. 62).

Only 11% of the world's soils can be farmed without irrigation, drainage, or other types of improvements (Singh, A., 2005) and this land has decreased 30% from 1961 to 1991 (Singh, A., 2005, p. 27). Iowa and Illinois have some of the best topsoil in the world and some of the highest crop yields. Iowa and Illinois are the largest corn producers in the U.S. The U.S. is the top corn producer in the world (see "World," 2014), so these states are important to global food sustainability. Iowa and Illinois also have some of the highest erosion rates (Singh, A., 2005). Conventional farming practices have been compromising the long-term sustainability of the land for decades.

It takes 500 years for one inch of soil to form under agricultural conditions (Singh, A., 2005, p. 27), and this can occur only if the farming practices are sustainable. Conventional farming results in net soil loss, soil compaction, and decreased organic matter content. Only no-till would allow for a net gain (Montgomery, D., *Dirt*). Iowa and Illinois have lost over half of their topsoil in less than 150 years (see "Iowa Soils," 2014). Lake sediments indicate that most agricultural erosion has occurred since intensive agriculture began in the 1950s (Heathcote et al., 2013). Thus, modern agriculture gives us less time to become more sustainable (see the following section on soil erosion and soil quality).

Other factors leading to global food shortages include political unrest, economic insecurity, urban development, and unequal food distribution (Singh, A., 2005, p. 28). All of these factors are expected to worsen with increased limitations on resources and population increases.

Food resource buffer   Corn supplies over 90% of the feed grain in the U.S. (see "Corn," 2014). Since the vast majority of the corn is used to feed livestock or produce ethanol, the potential to convert this land to feed people exists. This provides a substantial food safety buffer in case of limited resources. The percent of Iowa farmland planted as corn or beans is typically over 70%, and around 90% in about 25% of Iowa counties (see "Percent," 2004). The vast majority of our best farmland is currently unused for human food. Therefore, it remains an enormous buffer for human food production in times of scarcity as long as we take care of the soil. The buffer is very pronounced in the Midwest. However, it is also significant worldwide. Thirty-six percent of the world's crop calories feed animals instead of people (Foley, J., 2014). Thus, there is a global food buffer, not just an American food buffer.

For example, in 2012, 43% of the total corn crop was used for ethanol, 40% was used for animal feed, 4.5% was used for high fructose corn syrup, and 6.6% was exported (See "USDA,' 2014). If we consider that high fructose corn syrup is one of the worst things we can consume, almost 90% of the corn crop is for non-human food or for products we could do without.

A red meat diet is not essential. Land currently used to feed cattle could easily be converted to feed people, grow designer crops engineered with industrial conversion enzymes, grow crops engineered with renewable alternatives to fossil fuels, and the essential land management practice of allowing the soil to replenish itself by not cultivating it for a season. There is currently no systemic planning of soil replenishment for cultivated land which ensures that the net loss of soil will continue until such a policy is adopted. We have no systemic plan for replenishing our two most basic resources, soil and aquifer-sourced water. Soil is eroded and aquifers run dry if not managed correctly. Current practices and sustainability trends will ultimately leave a future generation with insufficient soil and water for survival unless better management takes place.

Using farmland for human food, designer crops, and replenishment would be far better management of the earth's arable land than its current use as crop production for cattle feed and ethanol production. Food sustainability may be more dependent on climate stability than land management. For example, most of the rich topsoil in the Midwestern U.S. is completely exposed in the wettest months of May and June as the fields are tilled intensively for planting. May and June have often brought torrential rains capable of eroding no-till fields. I have lived in the Midwest the vast majority of my life and watched downpours on mile after mile of fields that have no ground cover. The rains have become much heavier since my early years. If torrential rains on completely exposed soils continue, it won't take long to have an impact on yield. One possible way to stabilize the climate is by preserving what is left of the Amazon rainforest. The Amazon could be more easily set aside and left intact for climate stabilization and biodiversity if the demand for livestock and livestock feed were decreased or were met by non-forested land.

Soil erosion and soil quality Historically, the Midwest has had some of the highest soil erosion rates in the world (Singh, A., 2005; p. 27). Midwest land clearing was 95% complete by 1910, and Iowa is the most altered of the 50 states in the U.S. Seventy percent of Midwestern lands were drained by 1920. Agriculture intensification began in the 1950s. Intensive agriculture includes mechanization, fertilizer, biocide application, and increased farm size.

Erosion-sourced sediments in 32 Midwest region lakes have increased 75% since intensive agriculture began in the 1950s (Heathcote, A., et al., 2013).

Topsoil quality is decreasing. Topsoil before modern agriculture was much less dense allowing easier air and water movement than today's topsoil (Wolkowski, R., 2008). As mentioned, Iowa has overall lost more than half of its original topsoil since its conversion to farmland. Such obvious and critical changes should foster immediate and widespread action. Yet, soil erosion is not being monitored on a continual basis in a way that results in preserving the remaining soil. In addition to decreasing soil depth and quality, the land area per capita (hectares/capita) has decreased almost four fold since 1900 (Singh, A., 2005).

The complete exposure of Midwest farmland during the wettest months (May and June) will be of increased concern if torrential rain frequency increases roughly exponentially as the earth's temperature increases (Min, S., et al., 2011). Crop residue on tilled land is insufficient as a long-term means of reducing erosion. No-till is an effective method for reducing erosion to sustainable levels under normal rainfall conditions. (Montgomery, D., *Dirt*). However, even land with cover crops will not protect the land against torrential rains due to the flooding conditions created. During a drive through northern Iowa and southern Minnesota last June, I saw large areas where torrential rainwater had formed shallow lakes in the farm fields and washout gulleys on sloped no-till land. No-till cropland accounts for about 35% of total U.S. cropland. On the other hand, 65% undergoes some form of tillage (Horowitz, J., et al., 2010). The ground must remain covered year round in order to avoid net soil loss. Fortunately, agencies such as the National Resources Conservation Service are currently working toward developing strategies for continuous ground cover on cropland (see "NRCS," 2013).

Global Population Growth and Its Effects

Population projections and carrying capacity World population is projected to reach 8.1 billion in the early 2040s (Randers, J., *2052*, p.62); 8.9 billion by 2050 (Goodland and Anhang, 2009, p. 15). Jorgen Randers is one of the original authors of *The Limits to Growth*. According to Randers, "We are already beyond the physical carrying capacity of the globe" (Randers, J., *2052*, p. 72), but we do not yet experience the full effects. This delay in effect creates a false sense of security and it is a major factor in why population overshoot occurs (Randers, J., *2052*, p. xiv). Factors leading to delay in addressing overshoot include:

- The time required to identify sustainability problems.

- Time required for the general population to accept that sustainability problems exist.

- Time required to identify effective solutions to sustainability problems.

- Time required to implement effective solutions to sustainability problems.

All of these delays add up and can delay needed action to the point that the action is too late. There are examples of such overshoot events in animal populations.

Reindeer study on St. Matthew Island (Klein, D., 1968) In 1944, 29 reindeer were introduced by the U.S. Coast Guard to provide an emergency food source. The Coast Guard abandoned the island and left the deer. The carrying capacity of St. Matthew Island was approximately 13-18 reindeer per square mile, but the density of reindeer had risen to 47 per square mile by 1963 reaching a total population of about 6000, a 200-fold population increase. The winter of 1963-1964 brought one of the most severe winters on record. Astoundingly, less than 50 animals were left by the end of that winter. The cause of death was confirmed as starvation. Factors in the die-off included excessive numbers of reindeer and overgrazing of lichens, limited winter forage, and poor condition of the reindeer going into the winter.

Lichens were the most important winter forage. By 1963, lichen growth, formerly 8-12 cm deep, had been almost completely eliminated. The severe winter with deep snow restricted the availability of winter forage. Only one known male survived the die-off and that male may have been reproductively incapable. The population exceeded the carrying capacity by about threefold before the die-off.

Population growth and consumption A direct comparison cannot be made between a reindeer population and the human population. However, extreme events provide clarity on a few important points that apply to any animal population. Overconsumption combined with overpopulation is a deadly combination. Human consumption can be estimated by economic growth. If the average growth rate of the world economy remained at 3.5% (1970-2010 economic growth rate) until 2052, the world economy in 2052 would be more than three times as big as it is now (Randers, J., 2052). The following conditions are capable of creating a carrying capacity crash for humanity:

- If global human population has already exceeded the earth's carrying capacity. (Randers, J., 2052)

- If a threefold growth in the world economy over the size of the 2012 world economy results in a threefold resource consumption increase including food and water consumption.

- If cumulative effects of resource depletion result in carrying capacity overshoot of at least threefold.

- If carrying capacity actually decreases from now on due to resource depletion and environmental degradation.

- If resource depletion results in resource wars.

Unfortunately, none of these conditions can be eliminated from the realm of reality and neither can the combination of all of them. On St. Matthew's Island, environmental degradation had decreased the capacity of the population and it's habitat to cope with a climate change during the harsh winter of 1963-64. The earth as a whole is much more complex than St. Matthew's Island. However, if we deplete the global soil supply, we are capable of creating a carrying capacity crash because soil depletion affects almost all of the major crops. If we are capable of eroding over half of Iowa's topsoil in less than 150 years, we are capable of eroding the rest of it. Decreasing soil quality is another major factor because it will eventually result in lower yields.

Food scarcity aggravated by climate events, war, and pollution could bring about massive human die off events on earth. An exponential increase in extreme weather with global temperature increases has been predicted (Fischetti, M., 2013). Extreme rain on completely exposed soils will degrade them, and the degradation will increase with the extremity of the weather. More chemical supplements will be added to compensate for decreased soil quality. Cumulative effects of farm chemicals on ground water pollution could result in adverse effects on human health. Extreme drought is also expected to be part of future climate change patterns. Arid areas are expected to become drier. If we are forced to irrigate to maintain a sufficient food supply, freshwater supplies could be rapidly depleted.

The pace at which needed sustainability changes are currently taking place is most likely too slow to avoid the consequences of overshoot (Randers, J., 2052). For example, the switch to non-meat diets and renewables is already too late to avoid exceeding the 350 ppm carbon dioxide threshold established by NASA scientists for maintaining a stable climate. The level of carbon dioxide as of June 2014 was 401 ppm (see "Atmospheric," 2014).

Deforestation Most tropical rainforests have already been impoverished or converted to agriculture (Nepstad, D. et al., 2002). By 2002, only 15% of the Amazon had been deforested. Brazilian authorities had enacted regulations to direct the logging industry toward reduced-impact forest management. In spite of some advances, Brazilian government deforestation regulations do not appear to be capable of offsetting major economic drivers (Soares-Filho, B. et al., 2006). Deforestation rates depend largely on economic factors affecting local populations (Kaimowitz, D. et al., 2004). If prices to local peoples provide strong incentives for beef or crop production in the Amazon, rapid deforestation will resume. The amount of Amazonian forest remaining in 2012 was 81.2% (Watts, J., 2012). About 5% of the Amazon was lost in the previous decade. It is estimated that 40% deforestation will occur by 2050 (Soares-Filho, B. et al., 2006).

If the remaining tropical rainforests are not preserved, those genetic resources and associated problem-solving applications will be lost permanently. It would be a catastrophic loss of potential solutions and climate-stabilizing capacity. The loss of this vast genetic resource for the sake of a meat diet is not proper stewardship of the earth's resources. Many people actually prefer to risk these losses or deny its possibility rather than change their diet. International cooperation on management of natural resources is a requirement for long-term food sustainability. The international community should do whatever it can to help Brazil cap Amazon forest loss to less than 25-30%. One possibility is international funding of rapid screening of plant genomes and model plant systems in the Amazon in order to develop candidates for value added molecules in cover crops. Development of an economically lucrative cover crop for farmers could simulataneously help conserve soil in the Midwest and conserve the Amazon forest.

Landfills All landfills leak. According to Elizabeth Royte's book, *Garbageland*: "It is widely acknowledged, including by the EPA, that even the best plastic [liner] will ultimately leak and well before the waste it contains ceases to threaten the environment" (Royte, E., 2005, p. 57)." Even new landfills with modern liners can leak from the start. For example, a new landfill in Dixon, California, had an acknowledged 99.3% protection (Royte, E., 2005, p. 75).

Monitoring practices and regulations do not adequately address landfill leakage. Currently, the EPA requires landfill owners to monitor their sites for thirty years after closure. After this period, there is no funding for monitoring water and air quality or to remediate any pollution even though leakage increases after monitoring requirements end (Royte, E., 2005, p. 60). Landfills can leak for thousands of years, as those of the Roman Empire are doing today (Royte, E., 2005, p. 57), and they never stop posing a threat to the environment.

To protect groundwater and the surrounding environment long-term, a landfill must be recycled. Left to itself, landfill leakage will increase over time with unknown consequences. We are currently putting our most essential basic needs, food and water, at long-term, widespread risk. Landfills add to the long-term threat to clean water from energy practices such as fracking, agricultural chemicals, and other types of runoff. Every major urban area has massive landfills that will leak more with time. The size and widespread nature of landfilling is what generates the most concern.

We do not know the true cost of landfill leakage. The cost of cleaning future drinking water is not being considered now. Some water supplies in the future may end up so contaminated that it is cost prohibitive to clean them. If enough water supplies become unsafe and uncleanable, there will be insufficient access to clean water. The cost of inadequate access to clean water is paid in lives, not money. Risking drinking water for energy, unrealistically cheap products, and cheap waste disposal is the wrong risk to take. Future generations would tell us if they could. A bumper sticker from Northern Sun says, "Because we don't think about future generations, they will never forget us," and Albert Schweitzer said, "Man has lost the capacity to foresee and to forestall. He will end by destroying the earth" (Carson, R. *Silent Spring*).

We landfill because it is cheap, but our disposal costs do not reflect the true cost to ourselves and the environment. The true cost would include a product life cycle analysis that incorporates the cost of reusing or recycling the product and the product's environmental costs.

Sustainable Alternatives

Waste as a resource   Industry generates about 7.6 billion tons of solid waste per year (see "Guide," 2014) including chemical, iron and steel, plastic, resins, stone, clay, concrete, paper, and food waste. Consumers generated about 251 million tons of municipal solid waste in 2012 (see "Municipal," 2014), about 3% of the weight of industrial waste. Industry can make the biggest direct difference in waste generation and waste-handling, but only in conjunction with consumer demand. The relationship cannot be separated.

An excellent example is Interface, the world's largest manufacturer of carpet tile. Beginning in 1994, the company began to realize their vision of becoming the first company to incorporate sustainability in all its dimensions including people, products, process, and profit. Since then, waste from their carpet factories has dropped tenfold, water use has dropped sixfold, and carbon output has dropped threefold. In addition, 92% of their energy use comes from renewables (35%) or natural gas (57%). All of these are impressive, but the largest change was the 50-fold increase in use of recycled and bio-based raw materials (see "2013," 2014). Consumers have responded positively to Interface, and they are at the top of their field.

Consumers can create and maintain the demand for sustainability by choosing companies like Interface or by communicating their ideas for new products and processes to industry. Companies can choose short-term gain or long-term sustainability with their purchasing power. Companies can create their own long-term future by switching to renewable alternatives in products and energy use. Interface provides an excellent model for steady and significant change toward sustainability, and their success thus far has inspired a new vision. By 2020, Interface wants to have reduced their environmental impact to zero (see "2013," 2014). Innovators like Interface have invested in a long-term future. The failure of many companies to create a renewable and sustainable marketplace may jeopardize their own existence.

Landfill waste is a resource. The amount of industrial waste indicates that there is an abundant source of cheap raw materials waiting for innovative companies to utilize. Tons and tons of yard waste could be converted into energy or composted. Paper, construction, and food waste can be utilized. Even contaminated waste streams can be a resource if properly researched and handled. Companies can feed off their own waste or that of other companies and save money in the process.

All landfill biocarbon ultimately returns to the atmosphere as CO_2 or CH_4 as it decomposes. A study by Hatfield and Smith (2013) demonstrated the favorable carbon footprint of waste to ethanol systems utilizing agricultural waste streams due to the following factors:

- The absence of energy inputs to grow crops for ethanol production

- Carbon in the waste stream was captured by incorporating it into fuel, synthetic gas and stabilized carbon materials such as animal feeds.

- The use of residual heat from the waste to energy conversion process to reduce the heating costs of the manufacturing facility.

The true cost of products and services is the lifetime cost. As long as the lifetime cost of using and disposing of a product is not considered, we are unaware of the true cost. Some companies calculate and consider lifetime costs, but most do not. Consumers are almost entirely unaware of the lifetime costs of products and demand unrealistically low prices. This cost deferral is building up debt for a future generation to pay, and the cost will undoubtedly be too high.

Technological solutions   The main barriers that determine how public and private funding is spent are social, political, and personal. The finances and technology to address energy issues, preventative healthcare, and other priority areas exist, but the money has been spent elsewhere treating symptoms and accumulating profits to meet cultural standards.

Current technology and financial resources are sufficient to supply renewable electricity to the entire nation (Zweibel, K. et al., 2008). A solar network in the southwest could supply the entire nation with electricity for far less than the cost of the Iraq war (Zweibel, K. et al., 2008). If the public and political will was there, we would have renewable energy now. The initial cost of replacing fossil fuel technology with renewable technology is not high compared to spending in other areas. It is even cheaper if the cost to future generations is considered. Far sighted communities cut wasteful spending and invest the savings in future generations.

Many innovative companies and universities are developing renewable technologies that will eventually be economically competitive with fossil fuels. Because of the short-sighted nature of consumers and governments, we will have to wait for the market to allow these technologies to become widespread. Bloom Energy, for example, manufactures fuels cells for homes and businesses (see "Changing," 2014). Companies like Bloom envision a future where many homes are self-powered, renewable, and off-grid. This would create the highest possible level of energy security, air quality, and electricity-based carbon reduction. There would be no more threat of losing centralized power. As technology advances in both home-based power and batteries for electric cars, future home-based power could potentially produce producing your own energy for home and car! Cree is a company that manufactures LED bulbs and is planning to have a product priced competitively with traditional lighting in the near future (LaMonica, M., 2014). This is a major breakthrough given the current expense of most LED bulbs. LED bulbs last up to 30 times longer than comparable incandescent bulbs (Comstock, O., 2014).

Home-based power has similar implications for transportation. If technology develops to the point where renewable, home-based energy supplies generate enough power for home and car, we could eliminate electricity bills and significantly reduce our transportation costs. Electric car makers are breaking down driving-range barriers and cost barriers. As mentioned, Tesla will soon provide a long-range, competitively-priced electric car.

Because we have not invested in developing a renewable infrastructure, electric cars are not currently practical for long trips. However, Tesla's cars are practical for urban commutes, the biggest market.

Barriers are coming down in other areas. Intermittent power sources such as wind and solar have had storage barriers. Until recently, there has been no way to cheaply and reliably store utility-scale electric power for use when the sun stops shining or the wind stops blowing. Now companies like Ambri are developing batteries with inexpensive abundant earth materials that can handle utility scale power storage. Ambri is targeting battery costs below $500 per kilowatt-hour making it cost effective for utilities (LaMonica, M., 2014). Aquion Energy makes Aqueous Hybrid Ion, grid-scale storage batteries amenable to intermittent power generation (see "Aquion," 2014). The development of all these technologies could be rapidly increased by either market pressure or incentives. This is where government can provide opportunities for developing technologies by diverting symptom-money to solution-based investment. With the massive scale of symptom-money approaching over half of the federal budget, there is little doubt that large scale positive change would take place if the same funds were redirected to solution-based investments. Alternatively, consumers can drive change by their purchasing choices.

Biodiversity sustainability   The Amazon is the world's largest rainforest and the largest biodiversity resource. In terms of known species, about 10% reside in the Amazon (see "Amazon," 2014). In terms of undiscovered species, there could be thousands more. The genetic resources in the Amazon can provide solutions for many different types of problems including medicines, enzymes and proteins for biofuels, renewable resources, and many applications to be discovered. The Amazon is a problem-solving resource. According to Conservation.org, as many as two-thirds of medicines with known cancer fighting properties and 120 prescription drugs derive directly from plants in the Amazon (see "Amazon: Medicines," 2014). The potential resources in the Amazonian gene pool is far greater than what has already been discovered. Rapid screening technologies can help mine this vast reservoir of molecular diversity. Diversity in enzymes alone can provide industry with the tools to make more renewable, higher quality, much more advanced polymers, plastics, fuels, and foods. Very advanced molecular tools for regulating plant metabolism to generate "plant factory" model systems are likely waiting to be discovered. Currently, it is difficult to engineer agricultural crop species for overproduction of a renewable product. There is probably an undiscovered plant system that is much easier to engineer and scale up. If such plant systems are discovered, engineered, and scaled up, it will be possible to use plants to generate advanced renewable materials at low cost. Even more than the human genome project, this is a resource that deserves long-term, international funding to unlock its potential. Genetic resources can be accessed without destroying the forest and provide non-destructive income for locals.

Volunteer movement A volunteer movement is a sustainable approach to any type of crisis. Volunteers may not be able to solve every issue, but they can make a sustainable impact. The civil rights movement was a sustainable approach to a community issue. The environmental movement was a sustainable approach to a sustainability issue. In a crisis, cultural standards are challenged, people act, and policies change. People are less concerned with status during a crisis, and money becomes more a means to help others. In some types of crises, such as war, money can become virtually useless.

Communities are where the direct action and change takes place. Volunteers are mostly organized at the community level. Impacts on air and water quality occur at the community level. Managing and protecting water and air supplies is a community process. A volunteer sustainability movement is needed to maintain air, soil, and water quality for future generations. It starts at the local level and moves nationally like any other type of movement.

Environmental movement   The economic prosperity of the U.S. following World War II was not accompanied by laws that sufficiently safeguarded air and water quality. Raw industrial waste was piped directly into rivers and lakes. Cleveland received significant attention when its Cuyahoga River caught on fire in 1969. Lake Erie became so polluted that there were massive fish kills (Rotman, D., 2014). The pollution crisis raised public awareness to the level required for change. A single book, *Silent Spring* by Rachel Carson, led to the banning of DDT and very significant changes in environmental law. The environmental movement started in communities and moved to the national level. In 1970, the EPA and the first Earth Day were established (Gore, A., 1994). Like the civil rights movement, when enough people got involved, positive change came.

The Nature Conservancy   The Nature Conservancy (TNC) is the world's leading conservation organization with a membership of over one million and fundraising of about one billion dollars per year. The TNC is particularly impressive in its science and community-based approach to conservation. For example, it decides where to invest in land preservation by comparing factors such as biodiversity, cost, and community involvement. TNC works with local communities, industry, and governments through a comprehensive, science-based approach. Their management is outstanding. Mark Tercek came from heading the Goldman Sachs Center for Environmental Markets to become TNC's CEO in 2008 (see "Board," 2014). They recognize that working with people is the best way to conserve the environment long-term. For example, they worked with local fishermen, scientists, and governments in central California to adjust fishing methods so that they improved both the marine environment and the financial impact. Bottom trawling had resulted in a drastic decline in the fishery's economic performance. The multifaceted collaboration established by TNC is restoring the area for greater economic and environmental sustainability. This is an outstanding model for sustainability for several reasons. It involves diverse groups of people, diverse governmental agencies, and diverse areas of expertise. It established a successful collaboration between groups that traditionally clashed (see "California," 2014). This is the kind of complex approach needed for complex issues.

SNAP sustainability program TNC is applying a multifaceted approach such as that modeled in central California toward global environmental sustainability. TNC is collaborating with the Wildlife Conservation Society and the National Center for Ecological Analysis and Synthesis to develop a long-term sustainability program called Science for Nature and People (SNAP). SNAP's diverse approach includes integrating lawmakers, financial providers, and field practitioners. It will be based on the latest research carried out in a wide network of top quality labs. It targets areas of global significance such as preservation of the western Amazon ecosystem and agricultural productivity (see "SNAP," 2013).

Agricultural productivity and management changes in areas like the Midwestern U.S. can contribute significantly to relieving the pressure on the Amazon. However, no conservation program can address sustainability without addressing human behavior.

Individual Action Plans

Action items that are clear, easy to put into practice, and directly address sustainability such as reduced consumption and increased giving will have high impact if enacted by a sufficient proportion of the population. The vast majority of us consume more than we need and this can be reduced significantly for any person with excess resources. A similar situation exists with regards to giving back. Anyone who makes more than they need can give some of that back to the community and choose exactly where they want it spent. Small scale giving to conservation and community organizations by many people makes a difference. The situation is similar when many people reduce consumption. Fluorescent lights and mercury-containing thermometers are ubiquitous, and individual consumption choices can make a big difference. One gram of mercury (the amount in just two mercury thermometers) can make the fish in a 20-acre lake unsafe to eat (see "Mercury," 2014). Individual choice alone will not solve the mercury problem because coal burning power plants are responsible for half of the mercury pollution (Weise, E., 2012). However, home-based power together with LED lighting technology could someday address the issue.

Reduce, reuse, recycle Individuals can contribute much to environmental sustainability through the timeless sustainability hierarchy of reduced consumption, reuse of products, and recycling (the three Rs). People have control over how much waste they produce. I knew friends in graduate school who became a zero-waste household by applying the three Rs and cancelled their garbage service. It is a hierarchy, so reduced consumption has the greatest impact. Energy and material resources cannot be consumed if a product is never manufactured. Reuse involves only the energy and materials in the manufacture, distribution, and use of the product. Recycling adds to this the energy and materials used for recycling. Recycling is still valuable because it reduces the need for new raw materials. The three Rs hierarchy applies anywhere, anytime, to any community or business because consumption takes place wherever people live.

Consumption standards Cultural standards of consumption change. Rationing and recycling occurred in mass during World War II. Consumption standards increase during prosperous times. Many people are collectors of some sort. I am guilty of collecting instruments that produce a sound I want. I love music and have six guitars and four mandolins. Do I need them? I don't need them to live, but I would not be able to produce many of my songs without them. The songs would be lower quality without these instruments. I plan to use music gatherings and income to facilitate sustainability education for the common good, but there is a limit. Some collections don't contribute much to the common good because of their size and the nature of the items collected. Large collections of cars and coins would be examples.

Product demand Industry would not be able to generate as much waste as it does if consumers did not create demand for their products. In democracies, consumers have the power to create sustainable practices and processes with their buying power. As renewable alternatives enter the marketplace, consumers have the opportunity to drive industrial production in a sustainable direction. Consumers do not have direct control over what industry produces. However, consumers can drive trends with their purchasing power and speed up new product development with their choices. Rapid advances in computer technology have occurred because of consumer demand. It can happen again with energy or sustainable products. Consumer have the power to drive the development and market for electric cars, LED lighting, recycled paper, and many other products. Consumers need to step into their purchasing role in order for long-term sustainability to take hold.

Permanent Environmental Sustainability

Jesus came to redeem, transform, and recreate the world through relationships (John 6:51). A Creator who is relational by nature will redeem creation through relationships with His stewards (Genesis 2:15). He redeems people not only to redeem them, but also to use them to redeem earth. Even in the new creation, God will not do everything Himself. He will use people to renew the earth and rebuild cities (Isaiah 61:1-4).

"The Lord God took the man and put him in the Garden of Eden to work it and take care of it." (Genesis 2:15)

"The Spirit of the Sovereign Lord is on me, because the Lord has anointed me to proclaim good news to the poor. He has sent me to bind up the brokenhearted, to proclaim freedom for the captives and release from darkness for the prisoners, to proclaim the year of the Lord's favor and the day of vengeance of our God, to comfort all who mourn, and provide for those who grieve in Zion — to bestow on them a crown of beauty instead of ashes, the oil of joy instead of mourning, and a garment of praise instead of a spirit of despair. They will be called oaks of righteousness, a planting of the Lord for the display of his splendor. They will rebuild the ancient ruins and restore the places long devastated; they will renew the ruined cities that have been devastated for generations." (Isaiah 61:1-4)

"But here is the bread that comes down from Heaven, which anyone may eat and not die. I am the living bread that came down from Heaven. Whoever eats this bread will live forever. This bread is my flesh, which I will give for the life of the world." (John 6:50, 51)

Jesus anointed purpose from the Father was to redeem people first for their earthly purpose and then for their new creation purpose. The earthly purpose is a preparation for the new creation purpose (Warren, R., *Purpose Driven Life*). There will be fulfilling work for people to do (Isaiah 65:21) in the new creation (Wright, N.T., *Surprised By Hope*). They will participate with God in redeeming all that was destroyed in the present earth. Witnessing and participating in the recreation of cities tragically destroyed by human selfishness will be work that is full of hope and joy. All was not lost after all! God was in control the entire time! What seemed to be lost was only a small part of a much larger story. What we thought was lost forever is actually going to be redeemed forever and believers get to be part of the rebuilding process. This results in a complete change of perspective from earthly despair to hope.

Currently, we don't live sustainably on a global level because we don't live sustainably on a personal level. In the new creation, people will finally be personally sustainable because they will live in harmony with their Creator. The root cause of all environmental problems will be addressed completely and permanently. The door to decay will not be opened again. The chain of event that begins with unsustainable personal living will be broken. Thus, communities will be sustainable, perhaps to the point of precluding the need for financial dealings. People will freely give and receive as they have received from the Creator. There will be no poor or needy people. Everyone will be sustainably interdependent on the Creator and their community.

A fully restored relationship with the Creator in the new creation means that people will finally steward the earth's resources properly. There will be no more pollution, death, or decay. Energy will be non-polluting. Farms (Isaiah 65:21) will flourish and not degrade the soil. Water will be pure. We will witness the earth as it was intended to be when God first created it including old growth forests, pristine wetlands and prairies, oceans and skies all filled with wildlife. People will live in complete harmony with nature.

Permanent sustainability will only be achieved by the Creator himself in the following way. Fulfilling work will progress at maximum speed because people will not be limited by broken hearts, broken minds, and broken relationships. As a result, technology will far surpass what exists now (Alexander, E., *Proof of Heaven*). Energy and transportation will be efficient, renewable and non-polluting. Products will be designed with the end in mind, leaving nothing to waste. Agriculture will provide abundant food without depleting soil and water resources. This rebuilding will not be in vain. It will last because Jesus will be in charge, and, under His leadership, redeemed people will not have a desire to exploit natural resources. The restored creation will be so good that people will not remember the suffering of the present earth, even the worst kinds of suffering (Isaiah 65:16,17).

"Whoever invokes a blessing in the land will do so by the one true God; whoever takes an oath in the land will swear by the one true God. For the past troubles will be forgotten and hidden from my eyes. See, I will create new Heavens and a new earth. The former things will not be remembered, nor will they come to mind." (Isaiah 65:16,17)

Chapter 5

The Church as a Community Facilitator

The Church as a Community Facilitator

The church is a diverse body reaching out to a diverse community. It reflects the community in which it exists because its membership arises from the surrounding area. Because the church has the diversity of skills, experiences, interests, and resources found in its own community, it is the organization best suited to reach the community for the least cost. Churches are volunteer organizations containing a highly skilled and diverse workforce. No other organization can do what the church does for free. This is particularly relevant in a world where many nations are approaching unsustainable debt and unsustainable resource use.

The church is a facilitator. Its goal is better community. The need for sustainability work in times of decreasing resources and the ability to facilitate community interaction both point to the role of the church. The financial and social costs of government and political solutions are unsustainable, and the church can do the best job of leading sustainable reforms in preventative healthcare and welfare in the most cost-effective ways. The church is an army of volunteers, and volunteers are best suited for challenges that are financially unsustainable. Any path forward will be enormously expensive, but the cost of government programs are far higher. The church and non-profit organizations can get the job done at a fraction of the cost.

The church functions through giving of time, talent, and treasure. When people give out of a purpose-driven passion, the results exceed expectations. When people are driven by a high salary, results decrease dramatically. The corporate crises of recent decades were full of examples of guaranteed CEO packages gone horribly wrong. Hundreds of millions of dollars guaranteed to individuals who performed poorly or ran companies into the ground, such as Leman Brothers (Reich, R., *Aftershock*), Enron, MCI, Meryl Lynch, and AIG. Politics have been ineffective at bringing about sustainable change. For decades, we have witnessed demagoguery resulting in broken campaign promises. Voters that demand campaign promises are just as much a part of the problem as the politicians that make those promises. Demagoguery is a serious issue and it has become the norm. It has been justified necessary as a necessary evil of winning political campaigns. However, the large number of independent voters (42% currently, Jones, J. 2014) could indicate that people are weary of demagoguery and may respond to a campaign that honestly discusses the realities of our sustainability issues and asks for sacrifice to help address the problems.

A healthy church always has a culture that facilitates rather than divides. People who love and follow Jesus want to be like Him. Jesus was a facilitator. All types of people were drawn to Him because of His authenticity, radical insights, life-changing message, and diplomacy.

"And I, when I am lifted up from the earth, will draw all people to myself." (John 12:32)

Jesus was the ultimate example of a leader who could draw the widest diversity of people possible. This diversity is comprehensive and spans many categories, such as culture, national heritage, life experience, age, race, personalities, interests, skill sets, ministries, outreach groups, group diversity and strengths, and financial resources. God is determined to reach all peoples, and He has throughout history. Those of every nation and people group will be represented in His kingdom (Revelation 7:9).

"After this I looked, and there before me was a great multitude that no one could count, from every nation, tribe, people and language, standing before the throne and before the Lamb." (Revelation 7:9)

Why and How the Church is the Best Means to Bring Those in Need Together with Those with Resources

Healthy communities form when people help people. As previously stated, the church is the best organization to facilitate this process in the most cost-effective manner, because it is volunteer-driven and community-oriented by nature.

The role of the church as a servant of society Governments at all levels will not have sufficient funds to help everyone in need in times of economic and environmental crises. There are not sufficient government funds to pay for the recovery of every person that needs recovery. Free recovery programs are needed. Likewise, there are insufficient government funds to address the welfare and healthcare needs of a nation heading toward an obesity rate of two-thirds the population. Free preventative healthcare programs and strong employer incentives are needed.

The church specializes in handling the jobs no one else wants to do. This is its traditional role as a servant, and it is another factor that makes the church uniquely equipped for welfare and healthcare assistance. The church shines the brightest when it takes the unpleasant jobs. For example, Christians in the Roman Empire cared for those suffering from a serious plague in 251 AD and many of these caregivers died as a result. Obviously, no one but the church wanted that job. Many of those who could flee the plague left town including a famous doctor named Galen.

Christians cared for their pagan neighbors and relatives and nursed many of them back to health. Many came to faith as a result (Stark, R., *The Triumph of Christianity*).

It is not wise for well-resourced individuals to abdicate responsibility for caring for the needy to government agencies. This form of apathy or indifference is a society-wide time bomb. It is not wise for governments to exclude the church from helping communities meet healthcare and welfare needs. The U.S. has had one of the best records for cooperation between government, non-profit, and business sectors. It is perplexing that government has not increased its role in facilitating these interactions given the success of non-profit organizations in this country. There are hopeful examples. Many states including Illinois, New Mexico, California, and several others welcomed Celebrate Recovery into their prison programs because it works. The prison outreach is called CR Inside. It now has programs in all but eight states. This provides a model for effective interaction between the government, faith-based recovery programs, and churches.

Dysfunctional prisons have been known as places that governments and employees abandon. CR Inside is an excellent example of a faith-based volunteer organization taking on a job that no one else wants to do and doing it very well. This is what volunteers do better than anyone else, the jobs no one else wants to do. Something unexpected happens when people engage in the dirty work. They end up liking it because helping others helps them. The witness of being part of changed lives transforms the mentors and helpers of the world and gives them a higher level of desire for what they are already doing. Thus, it raises their impact even more. Mentoring for deep change is a job that few want to do, especially when they understand how much time and investment is required. Successful mentors are sacrificial servants because they invest years of hard effort in the lives of those they help. People lacking the commitment to change give up long before real change comes.

Another example of the role of the church in serving society is CCDA (Chapter 3). Few want to move from an upscale neighborhood to a poor, crime ridden neighborhood to do difficult, long-term work, but members of CCDA do this because of their Christian belief system. Grace, faith, hope, and love provide the theological basis and personal motivation for doing this difficult job.

Diverse community   A church naturally consists of people who have resources and those who do not. A community of people who know and care for each other is potentially a safer and more effective setting for meeting needs than government assistance. The caring and accountability levels would be high in any healthy church environment.

When a financial provider or care provider helps someone in need, a high level of accountability accompanies this process. No one gives their own money indiscriminately because they worked hard to earn it. Giving financially between individuals does not occur unless the terms of assistance have been clearly established. Even the most generous provider expects to see results. It works best if the provider has established the terms of assistance through a long-term relationship in which the provider is also a mentor. It is the long-term guidance of the mentor that makes the difference in whether financial assistance yields results. Thus, mentorship is the most important part of any accountability relationship involving financial assistance.

In order to change, people must commit to personal development and accountability because change is difficult and long-term. Financial assistance is virtually meaningless without accompanying life change. Oral Lee Brown (Chapter 2) makes 12-16 year commitments to students starting in first grade. She personally meets with each student over that time period and finances their college education. Because of her in-depth involvement that accompanies the financial assistance, the graduation rate is very high. The financial provider does not have to be the mentor. The provider can work through a team of people who directly mentor the individual in need. There are multiple options for setting up an accountability system.

Generous justice principles   No other type of organization has the theological basis (grace, faith, hope, and love) for giving the kind of effort required to address complex social issues such as poverty and injustice. Low level financial assistance combined with occasional counseling is insufficient to address poverty, homelessness, and other types of social injustice. Sustained mentoring relationships, sustained community relationships, sustained family relationships, financial support, case specific healthcare support, and basic needs assistance are needed to address the root causes of complex social issues (Keller, T., *Generous Justice*). The church matches people who have been through a complex and difficult life change such as divorce or bankruptcy with those who are currently going through it (Warren, R., *The Purpose Driven Life*). In fact, the church can provide not just one mentor for a complex problem but a group of mentors. The personal and social roots of poverty must both be addressed by groups of mentors to bring about sustained change. Celebrate

Recovery is perhaps the best example of this. Sponsorship is part of the foundational principles of CR, Principal 8 or Step 12. Why? Helping people helps us. We are in danger of relapse if we stop learning and passing along lessons to others.

Different skills and strengths   A church reflects the skills sets of the community it is in. Urban churches will have a large number of highly skilled and specialized individuals and the full spectrum of occupations whereas rural churches will have a more homogenous skill set relatively speaking. Skills are occupational. They can be learned through training and education. Strengths are more innate. Strengths are instilled in our biological and spiritual makeup by the Creator. *Strengths Finder* is an excellent tool for assessing innate strengths and focusing more energy on utilizing strengths than fixing weaknesses (Rath, T., *Strengths Finder 2.0*). Skills and strengths can work for or against each other. They synergize and multiply when they work together. They inhibit and stagnate when they work against each other. God gives us spiritual strengths as described in 1 Corinthians 12 for the common good. If we use them selfishly, they are a hindrance. Many other resources have thoroughly covered the topic of spiritual gifts (e.g. Blackaby, H. and Blackaby, M., *What's So Spiritual About Your Gifts?*).

Different experiences   Who can best help someone in need? Those who have been through a similar experience and learned from it are the best kind of help because they can provide empathy, support, and direction for those going through trials. A person who cannot understand or empathize with the person in need is not much help. For example, people who offer advice to trust God in the absence of understanding or empathy only make things worse for the person in need.

147

I sometimes experienced this during my career crisis in my 30s, and it made it more difficult to ask for help. Fortunately, God provided a series of understanding and skilled counselors who helped greatly. One counselor who was especially gifted in compassion helped through the most difficult relationships. He helped me let go of the resentment I held with the gentle admonition to "relinquish the quest" for their acceptance. Because I had come to know his compassion and care for me over the course of three years, I knew that the admonition was not a condemnation.

The church has a large number of people who have been through a difficult life event or series of events but made it through. Since recovery takes a lifetime for every human broken by sin (i.e. everyone), the maintenance phase of the recovery journey is just as important as the entrance into recovery. We cannot make genuine progress without the initial entrance into a restored relationship with our Creator through Jesus because the Creator is the required source of power and wisdom for lasting change. Likewise, we cannot experience a lasting and productive recovery without the maintenance phase. Once new life in Christ begins, it takes the rest of life to "work out our salvation" (Philippians 2:12). Humans need a combination of lifelong learning, lifelong recovery, and lifelong community. Biblical community is intended to meet all these needs.

Reprograming the old tapes that play messages in our heads is hard work for all involved, but the results are worth it. Understanding other people's recovery journeys helps us with our own journey. It doesn't require a lifetime to see significant results. Within four months of understanding that I had begun a loving relationship with God, my attitude and life began to change dramatically. Instead of dreading work, I looked forward to it. Instead of wanting to sleep in, I wanted to get up. Previously, I didn't want to get out of bed even for things I enjoyed doing such as photography. I still remember one of the first times I awoke without an alarm after years of wanting to stay in bed. I got up at five a.m. to take pictures in a national park. I thought, "Is this really happening?" One of the signs of depression is not wanting to do what we normally enjoy. I had always enjoyed photography but depression had robbed me of much of the joy of this activity. I knew something had changed when I woke up at five a.m. in Joshua Tree National Park excited about photography again, having no agenda other than to enjoy it. This kind of change is not uncommon. A friend who had a major struggle with pornography recently told me that he had no desire for porn after he came into relationship with Christ. The difference for him was unmistakable. Porn was part of horrendous spiritual attacks he experienced. When God set him free from those attacks, there was no going back. The change was immediate.

Different personalities Personality and interests help shape each person's role and mission in the community. Several modern personality assessments are available that accurately indicate personality strength areas that people can use to maximize their impact in the community. In addition, a personality assessment can help people avoid wasting time in areas of weakness. If a person does not have awareness of their personality strengths and weaknesses, their impact in the community will likely be reduced. Personality awareness helps us target needs more effectively. Personality awareness can also help people form more effective teams. Teams need complementary personalities to provide a broad spectrum of perspectives for problem solving. Teams become lopsided and ineffective when strengths and weaknesses are not balanced. A balanced team will have a greater impact in their community than an imbalanced team. However, personality is only one factor in a complex mix of characteristics and should not be overemphasized. For example, compassion is a manifestation of personality traits, interests, and experience. Any person can develop compassion no matter their personality. I know someone who is naturally a very strong "Type A" who developed high levels of compassion through life experience.

Different interests The Creator loves diversity. He made a wildly diverse universe. No two people are exactly alike. Identical twins illustrate this principle well. Two genetically identical people can have very different interests. One can be a farmer and the other can be a scientist. One interest is not better than the other, just different. The diversity of interests means that there is no need to copy. Each person has been given a unique set of interests. People usually have a combination of interests that are relatively unique. The Creator creates sets of interests as people's lives develop. Interests arise out of life experiences. Because interests are experience-based, they can be used to help others with similar experiences. No two people have exactly the same interest sets from the same experiences or information exposure. We have a unique biological makeup and that varies our interpretation of information and experiences. This guarantees uniqueness.

Unfortunately, we are capable of synchronizing our interests unnaturally through conformism. This is not God's intention for community. He wants to use each person's unique interests to form a supportive community that meets needs empowered by God-given interests and desires. As God dynamically creates our lives through experience, He creates interests that can serve others.

Different resources   Welfare in some form has existed for a long time, but its widespread expansion did not begin until the 1960s. The poverty rate at the beginning of the expansion was around 19% and falling rapidly. In 2012, the poverty rate was 15.1% and rising. About $12 trillion was spent on welfare programs by the federal government between 1964 and 2012, but the poverty rate never fell below 10.5% (Tanner, M., 2012).

If government welfare programs have not achieved the intended results, perhaps an alternative will. The Bible gives many examples of wealth redistribution in the church. Especially in Acts 2, the Bible described how believers shared everything. They even sold property to redistribute it to those in need. When people hold onto their wealth tightly, history has a way of interfering with that type of false security. If someone "builds new barns to store up wealth" God either gives them over to their heart's desire or takes it away through a crisis. Why? To save the soul of the wealthy person. Luke 9 makes the priority clear. "What good does it do to gain the whole world and lose our soul?" In other words, what good does it do to hold onto wealth too long? Wealth needs to be given away as it comes in because we never know when the opportunity to put it to use may be taken away. Many wealthy Christians understand this, such as R. G. LeTourneau, who practiced this principle by giving away 90% of his income as it came in (LeTourneau, R.G., *Mover of Men and Mountains*).

It's a joy to give. It is a joy to see our work applied in the community while we are alive to see it. There is a sense of satisfaction that our resources were well spent every time we make a difference in someone else's life. If we give away our resources as they come in, we are making sure that a significant portion of it is well spent. We can also take steps to ensure that our resources help others by setting up our wills to redistribute savings to high-impact recipients. One of the joys of giving is having the ability to give money exactly where we want it to go. If a person has a strong interest in child welfare, they can direct their resources to excellent organizations making the type of difference they want to make. They don't have to reinvent the wheel; working together with existing organizations is much more efficient. The diversity of organizations covers every major and most minor areas of need. There is no need to worry about funds going to waste. I have a will that specifies the distribution of my assets to several organizations including World Vision, World Relief, Nature Conservancy, and the National Alliance for the Mentally Ill. I feel a sense of relief every time I give to one of these organizations because I know that the donation will be used wisely.

The best of today's non-profits are run as well as or better than the best businesses, and it's not just the top organizations in their respective category. There are many excellent organizations in every major area of need. The abundant selection also allows givers to choose the location. A giver can choose a local, regional, or national organization. When we can choose to make a difference exactly where, when, how, and with whom we want, it's wasteful to not take advantage of the opportunity. If money is spent only on ourselves, we corrupt our own hearts with it. How does a person know if money has corrupted their heart? We all do this to some extent, but the more defensive a person gets about not giving or spending it all on themselves, the more they have corrupted their own heart through greed.

How the Church Can Use Its Diversity to Serve the Community and Help It Become Sustainable

Basic needs assistance Assistance with food, shelter, health care, and other basic needs must occur at the time of need. However, basic needs assistance does not address the life management issues often found as one of the roots of poverty and injustice. Basic needs assistance in combination with life management assistance has much greater potential to result in long-term recovery from economic and social injustice. There is an extensive network of existing organizations involved in meeting basic needs. Partnering with and helping serve and prosper these organizations is an efficient use of church resources. An excellent resource for providing more specific information for setting up food, housing and healthcare assistance in a way that helps instead of hurts the recipients is When Helping Hurts (Corbett, S., and Fikkert, B., *When Helping Hurts*). Basic needs assistance includes:

- Food assistance
- Housing assistance
- Health care assistance
- Employment assistance
- Community-specific needs

Celebrate Recovery for life management needs Christ-centered recovery ministry can help meet the life management needs of large numbers of people. Everyone needs recovery because everyone has a broken identity. Sin breaks our fellowship with God and thus our identity as well. Because our fellowship with God is imperfect and limited at some level by us, we cannot accept ourselves unconditionally on a consistent basis.

The identity indicators of fear and resentment reveal the brokenness in all of us. Thus, Celebrate Recovery (CR) can help everyone. For example, someone having trouble dealing with high stress levels at work would benefit greatly from CR even though they are not an addict. CR is a program that would help them manage stress at a foundational level by addressing identity issues. Without addressing the root, they will go through the same stress cycle every time they face a heavy workload. CR can help them address their stress in a long-term fashion and at a much deeper level. In fact, there are CR groups specifically for anxiety and depression.

Celebrate Recovery is particularly well-suited to handle large numbers of people in recovery. The Eight Principles and Twelve Steps address the core identity issues that drive addiction, anxiety, and depression. Anxiety and depression are the common colds of mental health. Many people experience some level of depression and anxiety. Most divorced couples have experienced significant depression and anxiety, but most do not seek twelve-step recovery programs to help them cope with the loss. Everyone is reluctant in the beginning to admit they need help with a mental health issue because of social stigmas. I remember being very reluctant to attend counseling for the first time because I thought it would make it harder for me to find permanent employment. It turns out that the opposite was true. When recovery principles are accepted and lived out, they lead surrendered people into a new identity in Christ. Identity recovery addresses the personal roots of poverty and injustice.

Maintenance phase of recovery needs a team The maintenance phase requires several experienced recovery specialists further along in their recovery journey. We would wear out one mentor in the maintenance phase; at least I know I would! It takes a community to successfully carry out the maintenance phase. The church naturally provides a team to meet the need. In 1 John 4:17, "Among us" indicates that experiencing God's complete love occurs through others in a community process.

"And so we know and rely on the love God has for us. God is love. Whoever lives in love lives in God and God in them. This is how love is made complete among us." (1 John 4:16-17)

Everyone needs a recovery team, but only some are aware of it. Many "strong" people who didn't need God have ended up finding God when their unsustainable paths came to an end. People who do not struggle with traditional forms of addiction still have socially acceptable addictions (food, entertainment, popularity, anger) that control their lives and keep them in bondage. A recovery team can handle such complex personal issues, and the diverse experience set in the church makes it well suited for this. A person can turn to the church body, which can provide helpers who are more advanced in their recovery for free. This is especially relevant for people who cannot afford specialists. God provided us with an effective, free alternative through the church.

Those who stay committed to long-term recovery stay recovered as long as they keep up with their daily recovery maintenance. Indeed, most people want to do their maintenance because the new life brought by recovery is worth the work. Some of the benefits of life-long recovery include strong accountability, lifelong growth, long-term community, and character that equips them to better handle future challenges. Recovery people know they can't live without Christ. They have lost confidence in their ability to control life and rely on God instead. This dependence makes them better equipped to handle uncertainty.

Mainstream recovery Recovery ministry in the mainstream of church life creates an environment in which people come to church for help with problems. The rise of economic and relational instability may increase the number of mainstream people entering into recovery. We need others the most when we are hurting, and Celebrate Recovery provides a caring community where people can heal.

Many evangelical churches, until recently, have not encouraged transparency with problems. People who need recovery are reluctant to share problems in an environment where people hide problems. Recovery ministry is better suited than any other means to transform churches into safe places for recovery where vulnerability is encouraged and hiding is discouraged.

Future recovery needs An increasing proportion of society will need the tools of Christ-centered recovery. People from broken relationships are seeking recovery. People with broken dreams are seeking recovery. Career changes are major life events that lead people into recovery. Recovery program members can help meet the needs. Free community-based recovery has the potential to effectively help more people than any other type of help. People in recovery programs can be equipped to seek out those in need and invite them into the program. The potential number of helpers is limited only by the willingness and ability of people to recover and help others. Christ-centered recovery offers real hope for personal growth. People will need the hope God offers more than anything else if resource-limiting times arrive. Earthly life will not have much to offer the masses in times of limited physical resources.

How the Church Has Made a Difference Historically

William Wilberforce was widely involved in community service in addition to his main mission of bringing slavery in England to an end. His involvement with community service included campaigns against bull baiting, against child labor, and for penal reform. He was involved directly or through friends in the establishment of societies for Support and Encouragement of the Deaf and Dumb Children of the Poor, the Society for Bettering the Condition and Increasing the Comfort of the Poor, the British National Endeavor for the Orphans of Soldiers and Sailors, the Institute for the Protection of Young Girls, and many other organizations. A key group involved in establishing these organizations was called the Clapham Circle. It consisted of committed Christians who worked with and through their churches (Metaxas, E., *Amazing Grace*). Churches have historically started hospitals, schools, missions, shelters, mentoring organizations, and other types of faith-based non-profits that provide food assistance, health care, housing, and other needs. Given the number and diversity of these types of faith-based organizations, the church has made a major impact on community service throughout its history. This area has been covered more extensively by other resources.

Churches Making a Difference Today

Saddleback Church is an example of a church using a comprehensive, multifaceted approach to caregiving. For example, it addresses personal sustainability through Celebrate Recovery and several other church ministries. It is the church that started Celebrate Recovery. It addresses community sustainability through its PEACE Center. Within recent years, it distributed 1,025,000 pounds of food, helped 1225 people with health insurance applications, trained 202 people in CPR and first aid, instructed 705 students in English as a second language, and helped initiate 220 new faith journeys for a total of 19,610 people served with 29,725 volunteer hours (see "The PEACE Plan," 2014). Saddleback has also been the major force behind the transformation of Rwanda so much so that many other nations have come to Saddleback for help in transforming their governments (Warren, R., 2014). One church helping an entire nation is a good ratio!

The Willow Creek Care Center at Willow Creek Church also takes a comprehensive approach. Its services include immediate assistance with food, children's clothing, housing, transportation, and long-term guidance for education, employment, healthcare, legal services, and financial services. The Greater Chicago Food Depository honored Willow Creek with one of its Quality Performance Awards (see "Our Services," 2014).

The histories of some successful Christian organizations can be found at the following websites:

World Vision provides comprehensive caregiving using multifaceted approaches:

http://www.worldvision.org/about-us/our-history

World Relief provides comprehensive caregiving using multifaceted approaches:

http://worldrelief.org/history

Celebrate Recovery
http://www.saddleback.com/celebraterecovery

How to Help Your Church Become a Difference Maker in the Community

There are abundant opportunities for church members to partner with others in their church, with other churches, and with non-church organizations and businesses. The most efficient way to do this is for people to find a good fit with their interests, experience, skills, and abilities. Chances of finding a strong fit are excellent because there are so many high quality businesses and organizations involved in the community.

Some churches partner with a set of other organizations that are compatible with their own mission. My church, Lutheran Church of Hope, partners with Wildwood Hills Ranch, Meals from the Heartland, Freedom for Youth, and Joppa homeless ministry to promote these organizations and provide volunteers and financial resources. Wildwood Hills Ranch helps about 1,000 at risk youth every year and makes a ten-year commitment to each young person. Meals from the Heartland packages over five million meals every year for people in need globally. Ten million meals were packaged in 2014. Freedom for Youth reaches out to youth in an economically depressed area of Des Moines, and Joppa brings supplies to homeless people. Most of these organizations were started by members of Lutheran Church of Hope.

Every urban area has churches that partner with a variety of ministries and organizations. The usual barrier for members getting involved is not opportunity but priorities. The compelling rationale for making community service a priority emerges from the urgency to become sustainable as individuals and communities. Healthcare and welfare have the highest impact on personal, community, financial, and ultimately, environmental sustainability.

Once someone finds their niche, makes it a priority, and becomes involved, expansion is the next step. Expansion can involve increasing the level of time or financial commitment and recruiting other members of the church or community to join them. This is an important step because long-term community sustainability requires at least 50% significantly involved in community service. The Bible indicates that God originally intended 100% community service involvement.

Action Items

All of the action items for "Investment Priorities for Community Sustainability" at the end of Chapter 6 are relevant to the church. Please refer to this list.

Chapter 6

Everyone Needs to Serve

Why Communities Need Everyone to Serve

As mentioned in the Introduction, repetition of important sustainability themes in this book is intentional in order to reinforce the lesson of the interdependence of the different types of sustainability. The Introduction also mentioned that there is one main take home lesson from the entire book: that everyone needs to do their part to better the community in order for our communities to become sustainable. Long-term sustainability is not the current trend in our communities. If we are to become sustainable, it will be a movement by the masses working together. Practically speaking, we know that everyone will not do their part for sustainability. However, if we achieve at least 50% of citizens fulfilling their role in sustainability, we have a good chance at maintaining a sustainable society overall.

If more than half of the population are living sustainable lives, the potential exists for the sustainable half to help the unsustainable half. If less than half of the population are living sustainably, then the scales will begin to tip toward overall unsustainability. People lacking a sustainable level of skills and resources can't help others. Thus, at least 50% of the population must be personally and financially sustainable in order to ensure a resource pool big enough to maintain community sustainability. In 2011, 64 million U.S. adults (about 26%) volunteered (see "Charitable," 2014). A higher level of strategically targeted volunteerism is needed for long-term, sustainable communities. There are many people who volunteer but it is not strategic or extensive in most cases. Usually, it involves an occasional event based on social or work involvements. Strategically targeted volunteerism would prioritize the biggest personal sustainability targets such as obesity and addiction since all other areas of sustainability are dependent on human behavior.

Some may argue that far less than 50% personal and financial sustainability would get the job done since the wealthiest people could potentially sustain a large number of people or for other reasons. However, this does not work well in practice. Wealth in the hands of a few individuals cannot be easily distributed. Just as the economy is more stable when wealth is voluntarily distributed among the masses by the free market system as from 1945-1975 (Reich, R. *Aftershock*), communities are more stable when the masses help each other. The 1945-1975 distribution of wealth was an example of the masses helping the masses economically. The wealthy can't stimulate the economy by spending money on themselves because they literally have too much money. There are only so many houses, cars, and boats a wealthy family can use. However, they can help stabilize economies and communities by spending it on community programs and projects that benefit others.

The top 1% of the wealthy have so much money that they can impact the masses by distributing it through existing organizations or starting new organizations. Many wealthy families do give their excess away and start foundations and non-profit organizations. The Arthur M. Blank Family Foundation, for example, focuses on innovative solutions to improve the lives of youth and their families. Specific programs include early childhood development, education, the Inspiring Spaces program which supports the development of parks, and the Art of Change program which funds programming for music and the arts. One of the innovative health initiatives was a meal program at Woodward Academy in Atlanta that serves nutritious, gourmet style food to students to encourage healthier eating habits. Students are eating healthier because the food is delicious and highly nutritious (see "Making," 2014).

This type of wealth distribution can get the resources to the needy population effectively and accountably. Experienced community service organizations know which clients are ready to accept assistance responsibly and which are not. As mentioned, people are generally not helped by assistance without accountability. There are some exceptions. It is actually much more cost effective to help people on the extremes of homelessness, mental illness, and addiction than to not help them. This is due to the cost of policing and hospitalizing these individuals (Gladwell, M., *What the Dog Saw*). According to the Housing First initiative, quickly providing housing to homeless individuals without conditions saves the system considerable costs because most clients need "surprisingly little support or assistance to achieve independence (see "Housing First," 2014)." This approach works financially and the compassion of initiatives like this has a positive effect. However, it only addresses part of the problem. Humans by nature need lifelong comprehensive and intensive care administered through relationships with God and community to become truly healthy.

The financial savings in caring for the least reflects the value of compassion. I helped with a breakfast at the Downtown Emergency Service Center (DESC) in Seattle, where such a program was working and saving the city millions of dollars. People with chronic mental illness and substance abuse issues were provided housing and community programs. DESC helped almost 7,000 people in 2013 (see "Supportive," 2014). People had been taken from the misery of homelessness and given a second chance at dignity. It was obvious as we observed and talked to the breakfast clients that DESC was a better alternative than the street, even if many would not be able to hold jobs or overcome their issues. Sometimes, compassion doesn't fully make sense, its value in creating a more civil society is unquestionable. Many of us, including myself, were only a few short steps from homelessness. Had I seriously injured myself in an attempted suicide, I could have easily ended up homeless. Then, I could only hope for a program like DESC to help me out.

Why People Need to Serve

People have a built-in need to serve. God designed us to serve in order to become more like Him: unconditional. The process of transformation is one in which we are continually becoming more conditional or less conditional, more selfish or less selfish, more like God or less like Him. Becoming more like God involves reflecting more of His image out of a desire to be like Him. To become more like God is to become more unconditional, the trademark of His love. God is the only One who can claim to be the source of unconditional love, and we receive it from Him. The practical manifestation of unconditionality is serving others who can't or won't pay us back. Serving others reinforces unconditional love and heals our identity in the process. Serving is a basic life need.

Unconditional thoughts and acts free us from fear and resentment. For example, helping at a homeless shelter was the act that lifted my depression the most during my career crisis. Sometimes I forget the power of serving others and start to isolate myself in pain again. I felt it happening to me recently. I was feeling judgment from others, resented it, and started avoiding people. I had forgotten that, in these situations, all I needed to do to overcome my resentment was to start serving someone,

---

165

especially the offender. I've experienced this many times in life. Serving overcomes resentment and fear. As we become more unconditional, we become less selfish. As we become less selfish, we become more joyful. As we become more joyful and grateful, we become healthier spiritually and physically. Healthier people are more productive, more connected with God and others, and more connected with their purpose. This is why we have a biological and spiritual need for serving. It keeps our dark sides at bay.

Fear and resentment have negative physical and spiritual consequences on us. They cause very damaging forms of stress that can eventually lead to heart attacks and strokes (Goleman, D., *Emotional Intelligence*) . Fear and resentment result in conditional acts done with the expectation of getting something in return. We selfishly look to others to give us something to heal our identity, but things like status, money, or popularity can't satisfy us. Unconditional love is the only thing others can give us that actually helps heal us.

Communities Need Everyone by Design

Communities are like teams. To be effective, teams must have diverse perspectives and abilities. This diversity in skills, talents, and experience is needed to handle the diversity of needs and problems in any community. It is well known that teams consisting of individuals that are too similar cannot handle unforeseen problems as well as teams consisting of a wide diversity of people. People that think alike will have a more limited set of possible solutions than a diverse team when problems arise. Multiple perspectives and unconventional thinking are needed to address previously unknown issues. Communities, churches and schools are naturally diverse which means that they already have a diverse skill and experience pool that can be used as a resource for problem solving. Communities don't thrive unless people use their unique makeup to serve each other. Problems predominate over solutions in communities that don't work together. Conversely, communities that work together solve problems. People with different belief systems can find common ground based what they care about (Swanson, E., and Williams, S., *To Transform a City*, Chapter 8). Community shelters are great examples of neighborhood residents coming together to solve a problem. Food banks are another example of community and church-based problem solving. They exist in every major community and enlist the help of volunteers to help under-resourced families. At the simplest level, providing nutritious food is one of the easiest problems for regular citizens to solve from the provider standpoint. America has abundant food and many people garden. Ample Harvest (ampleharvest.org) links local producers and those purchasing food to donate with food banks in any area of the US (see "Gardeners," 2014).

Communities are diverse and team-oriented by design. God intended this diversity so that healthy communities could work together to address their issues. The wide diversity of skills and experiences indicates that communities already have a deep pool of resources for addressing problems. The level of complexity this resource pool is able to address increases in proportion to the depth of the resource pool. Thus, almost any large city has the potential to solve its own problems with its existing resources. Resources are not usually the main obstacle. Insufficient levels of cooperation between community stakeholders is a much larger problem. Cooperation is ultimately dependent on personal sustainability issues.

The biblical way to conquer earthly problems is intended to be mediated through God's unconditional love (Romans 8:37) – the opposite of power struggles. It is the power of service and humility. Problems get solved when God fills people with unconditional love because God's love breaks down relational barriers. When relationships are healthy, people can work together and accomplish much. God resolves issues in the world through unconditional, counter-cultural love, a love that breaks down the idols that break relationships and communities apart (Romans 8:37).

"No, in all these things we are more than conquerors through him who loved us." (Romans 8:37)

Why Masses Helping the Masses is Better Than Welfare

Masses helping the masses can take place through widespread volunteerism among existing or new organizations or by helping neighbors. Masses helping the masses is more effective than federal aid because it is relationally based. When people know the people who are helping them, there is inherent accountability. Financial assistance accompanied by a healthy long-term relationship is a powerful incentive for positive change. Community members helping each other also allows diverse community teams to form and provide the broad skills, experiences, and relationships necessary for the comprehensive care humans require.

Since food, healthcare, and shelter are basic needs for every person, we need many more comprehensive care facilities in every metropolitan area and in rural counties.

Fortunately, this is practical for ordinary citizens to do, since feeding, housing, and providing basic needs for people is fairly straightforward. People with different faith backgrounds or no faith background can work together as volunteers in community organizations and in the workplace. They can form teams to build a house, stock a food bank, or start a shelter. Residents of the Lincoln Park neighborhood in Chicago came together in 1985 to form Lincoln Park Community Shelter (LPCS) in response to their concern about the increasing number of homeless individuals. A partnership between four different churches helped make the shelter a reality. More than 1,500 volunteers from a wide variety of faith and non-faith backgrounds help the shelter with meals and overnight supervision each year. The shelter's On Track Program helped more than 70% of clients gain housing and remain stable two years later (see "Fiscal," 2014).

The comprehensive services LPCS provides has continued to expand. In 2013, they launched Independent Community Living, LLC, which offers a housing subsidy and social services to highly vulnerable individuals who are homeless and disabled. LPCS also added on-site employment services which allows clients to be referred to open positions through a job developer and improved credit through a credit coach (see "Fiscal," 2014). All of this began with a group of concerned residents!

Welfare can't offer this local, long-term commitment and accountability. The long-term relationships between people with skills and resources and people in need is a major part of what makes LPCS such a success. For too long, welfare high-rises concentrated the poor and vulnerable people and facilitated their isolation from outside help. This isolation made many poor families vulnerable to gangs who took advantage of the situation.

The poor need a diverse community where those residents with resources and skills mix freely with those in need. LPCS demonstrates that ordinary citizens can make a comprehensive difference in the lives of the most vulnerable without getting too complicated.

Whenever people at the local level give resources, skills, and time to someone in need, they expect a return on their investment in terms of changed lives. The time investment needed to actually help someone move toward lasting positive change is measured in years. If people in need are making progress, their mentors need to stick with them as long as it takes to achieve sustainability. People don't regret this type of investment. The more time they invest, the greater the reward when lives change. The return from a changed life is more valuable than any financial returns.

Few engage in this type of provider relationship because it is complicated, long-term, and problematic. However, the absence of these types of relationships and resulting abdication of this responsibility to the government has resulted in less stable communities prone to violence and unrest. The short-term ease of the masses not entering into accountable relationships with those in need has brought long-term instability that ultimately affects everyone, including those who abdicate this responsibility. Accountable community relationships are worth the cost in the end.

Masses Helping the Masses through Recovery

Healthcare, welfare, and recovery issues have the greatest impact on personal and community sustainability, and have the greatest potential for future growth. There is much room for growth in welfare and healthcare volunteerism. The top volunteer activities in 2011 included food collection and distribution (24%), general labor or transportation (20%), and tutoring (18%). Within these categories, only 14% of volunteers were involved in social services and 8% were involved in health organizations (see "Charitable," 2014). As mentioned, non-prioritized volunteerism has not been strategic enough to sufficiently impact sustainability. Volunteerism has also not been holistic enough. For example, disaster relief efforts help those in need but leave behind a sea of single use containers and other garbage that end up in landfills. Too much of wreckage and packaging material left after a natural disaster is landfilled instead of recycled. The waste from hurricane Katrina could have filled three Superdomes (see "Hurricane," 2011).

Healthcare, welfare, and recovery are the best places to start getting involved in the community because, ultimately, these are the areas that have the greatest impact on every other area of sustainability including environmental sustainability. When people serve together, people change each other for the better. Organizations such as the Giving Pledge (story below) validate how much giving changes the providers, and organizations like Lincoln Park Community Shelter validate how much giving helps those in need.

Mental health   According to the National Institutes of Health, about 26% of Americans over age 18 have a diagnosable mental disorder (see "The Numbers," 2014). The most common disorders have been anxiety and depression. An estimated 18% of Americans over 18 have an anxiety disorder. Anxiety disorders often occur simultaneously with a depressive disorder or substance abuse. Major depressive disorder is the leading cause of disability in America for those ages 15-44 (see "The Numbers," 2014). In spite of the widespread nature of anxiety and depressive disorders, the main mental health burden is concentrated in about 6% of the population over 18 who are seriously ill.

Obesity and food addiction   Due to the broad scope of obesity, it is an area where everyone can make a contribution. All of us are either overweight, obese, or have friends who are. According to Gary Taubes, co-founder of the Nutrition Science Initiative, the trends in obesity, diabetes, and their complications are the "most critical health issue of our era" (Taubes, G., 2013). They have the potential to overwhelm healthcare, welfare, and financial systems. The current obesity rate is over one third of Americans. The rate has doubled in less than 40 years, and the increase correlates with the rise in the availability of fast food and sugar-laden foods.

If we revisit the series of shocking statistics from Chapter 3 that clarify the seriousness of the type 2 diabetes epidemic, the numbers illuminate the path forward in addressing it. All of us can consider the following and take action:

Prediabetes
- 86 million (35%) currently have prediabetes and 90% of these individuals don't know they have prediabetes.
    - 15-30% of prediabetics will develop type 2 diabetes within five years.
    - *Action item*   Ask at-risk individuals if they have been tested for diabetes and if they know the risk timeframe.

Diabetes
- 29 million (9%) currently have diabetes
    - Medical costs for people with diabetes are twice as high.

o *Action item* Ask at-risk individuals if they are aware of the cost risks.

o Risk of death for people with diabetes is 50% greater.

- People with diabetes are at higher risk for the following serious health complications.
  o Blindness
  o Kidney failure
  o Heart disease
  o Stroke
  o Amputation of toes, feet, or legs
  o *Action item* Ask at risk individuals if they are aware of the secondary health risks.

Prevention

- Type 2 diabetes is preventable and reversible in many cases by doing the following action items:
  o Lose 5% or more body weight (www.cdc.gov/diabetes/prevention)
  o Eat healthy (Warren, R. et al., *Daniel Plan*)
  o Increase exercise (Warren, R. et al., *Daniel Plan*)

People with diabetes can also manage the disease better with the above actions.

Financial Management for the Common Good

Balancing tax rates Financial sustainability is probably the most practical reason people need to help people. Americans vote mainly for economic reasons. If we could see or experience the long-term national financial consequences of not helping people, most would probably increase their community involvement significantly simply for its practical significance to their own financial stability.

Proportional taxes as mentioned in Chapter 2 should have conditions on both ends. Options could be given to the taxpayer to pay taxes in the form of community investment. The government could recognize community agencies that contribute to community sustainability based on objective criteria and then recognize taxpayer contributions to projects that save the government money as tax. It would be a recognition of investment that the government no longer needs to make. Chances are very good that this kind of community investment would yield far better results than programs administered by the government. On the government end, agencies at the state and federal level that do not manage tax income well based on objective criteria should have restrictions on any additional funding or cuts in funding until the agency meets the criteria. Illinois, for example, has the worst record for financial management. Tax increases did not result in effective debt management because financial management fundamentals are in disarray (see "Illinois Drowning," 2014). Since pension funding makes the largest contribution to debt mismanagement, that revenue stream needs restrictions.

Giving to charity   The top 1% of income earners in the U.S. have 34% of the total wealth and the top 0.1% had 15% of the total wealth. The top 1% captured 95% of the income growth from 2009-2012 (Rotman, D., 2014). The scope of the impact that the top 1% of the wealthy and the top 1% of wealth earners in every community, large and small, can make on our communities is relevant to everyone. Their collective buying power could impact every community in significant ways if it is invested strategically. The wealthy can fund comprehensive care centers in every community. Through these centers, the providers in collaboration with volunteers and employees have the buying power to provide access to programs that target the top personal sustainability needs that affect all other areas of sustainability.

The wealthy can have very high impact in the community now by investing it in long-term solutions with highly reputable, existing organizations. The accountability to ensure the impact of individual investment is driven largely by the desire to help people and the desire for maximum return on investment. No one who has effectively managed their money wants it to be wasted. The responsibility lies with everyone, not just the wealthy. The emphasis here is that the wealthy can make a very significant and immediate impact. However, by not investing in the community now, wealthy individuals are lowering the potential impact of their resources. If they do not invest it while they are alive, they abdicate responsibility for the community impact of those resources to someone else. It is well known that this approach does not always work well. Poor succession planning can lead a company into bankruptcy if the next generation of leadership is not sufficiently prepared and motivated.

Another potential wealth waster is a high level economic crisis which can decrease the value of currency and lower the community impact. For example, the dollar can still have high impact in many developing countries overseas due to the exchange rate. If this ratio were to drop tenfold by a devaluation of the dollar during a crisis, it would roughly correspond to accomplishing tenfold less while keeping all other factors constant. In this sense, wealthy people can help ten times as many people if they invest now. Investing now ensures a high return on their investment because they can drive results and take advantage of the dollar's favorable status. The Gates Foundation is taking advantage of this principal with their malaria work in Africa (see "Malaria," 2014).

Direct investment in the community by the wealthy
Comparing taxes with giving is difficult because people like Bill Gates, Warren Buffet, and John Maxwell spend their money in the community far better than the government. Do we penalize them to help our debt situation? It is probably better for the generous rich to show the not-so-generous rich what a difference they could make in the community. Direct investment in the community by the wealthy is the most effective route as long as the government manages the debt irresponsibly. Because elected leaders have not managed debt well, a compromise such as a conditional 50% top tax rate is better than historically high top tax rates as long as the wealthy invest in the highest priority areas that impact sustainability. It is very possible that historically high top tax rates would be needed to deal with sustainability issues, but this would only work if the tax revenue were directed to high priority sustainability targets. Sustainability conditions should govern both taxation and spending in order to address both debt management and community sustainability needs. One way or another, taxation and spending conditions that lead to sustainability would result in at least 50% of the top wealth being invested in prioritized sustainability targets. Poor management of the debt leaves us unprepared for a variety of situations, such as an energy crisis, a climate crisis, or war.

Giving is a privilege. History provides examples of societies where people did not have the opportunity or the resources to make a difference. Oppressive communist governments took away wealth and lives in Cambodia (Cormack, D., *Killing Fields Living Fields*). Similar events occurred in other communist revolutions. In China, the communist policy of banning of private farms in 1958 resulted in the mass starvation of about 45 million people

(Talbot, 2014). Poor countries have few individuals with excess resources. We live in a free country and wealthy individuals have the opportunity to direct how their money is spent. If wealthy individuals and organizations have the resources to put long-term sustainability into effect, why not invest in the community now? The collective individual resources within America can have immediate, large-scale impact with existing organizations. The best time to invest excess wealth is while it can still be invested for maximum impact. Those with wealth must invest it before a crisis. Community investments made according to prioritized sustainability targets would reduce the chances of a future crisis.

Wasting wealth is probably in the minority of cases. For example, Elvis managed his money so poorly that he ran out and had to do concerts or movies to pay his bills. His enormous wealth may have been wasted if others had not helped (Maxwell, J., *Thinking for a Change*).

Hoarding wealth is common. Most people do not give significant percentages of their income. Middle class household earning $50,000 to $70,000 gave a much higher percentage of their income on average, 7.6%, than those earning more than $100,000, who gave 4.2% (Gipple, E., and Gose, B., 2012). Among individuals worth $10 million or more, the reasons for not giving were not inspiring. These reasons included needing a higher level of confidence that their wealth would continue to support their lifestyle and family, needing improvement in the markets, and finding something they could be more passionate about (Frankl, R., 2013).

Over 90% of high net worth households give to charity (see "Charitable," 2014), but it appears that there are only a few of the wealthy doing most of the work in terms of proportionate giving. In 2010, Bill Gates and Warren Buffett initiated the Giving Pledge in order to encourage America's wealthiest families to give at least half of their wealth during their lifetimes and write a letter saying why. The letter from Bill Ackman is an excellent example of the link between personal, community, and financial sustainability. He writes:

"The emotional and psychological returns I have earned from charitable giving have been enormous. The more I do for others, the happier I am. The happiness and optimism I have obtained from helping others are a big part of what keeps me sane. My life and business have not been without some decent sized bumps along the way, and my psychological health and wellbeing have made managing these inevitable challenges much easier" (Ackman, B., 2010).

It is possible that the fastest way to manage the debt is by changing lives. Several millionaire or billionaire community investment groups already exist. These groups can recruit by example. Good examples are hard to resist. My dad was a great example of a consistent giver and it was only natural to follow it. Recruiting the wealthy as givers may be as easy as showing them a new community center like the Care Center at Willow Creek church. It's a beautiful building housing an award-winning program that makes a big difference in the community. One of the Giving Pledge billionaires indicated that the example of others, especially his father, had helped him to become a better giver: "I don't think being charitable is innate. In my experience, it is learned from the example of others" (Ackman, B., 2010). Supporting this is the finding that wealthy people living in more diverse neighborhoods gave more than those living in neighborhoods with other wealthy people (Gipple, E., and Gose, B., 2012).

Community values transfer when people in community connect. The community connections made through giving are also good for business. According to a letter from the Giving Pledge:

"While my motivations for giving are not driven by a profit motive, I am quite sure that I have earned financial returns from giving money away. Not directly by any means, but rather as a result of the people I have met, the ideas I have been exposed to, and the experiences I have had as a result of giving money away" (Ackman, B. 2010).

The Giving Pledge currently has 127 participants that include Michael Bloomberg, Larry Ellison, Ted Turner, and Mark Zuckerberg (see "Pledger," 2014). The Giving Pledge billionaires engage in open dialogue about giving more, giving sooner, and maximizing their impact. They hope to shift social norms about giving to this model rather than leaving excessive wealth to inheritance. They interact throughout the year to discuss challenges and share ideas on how to tackle complex problems such as poverty, healthcare, and human slavery (see "Frequently," 2014). These individuals are highly skilled managers that know how to invest wisely. Together, their skills and resources can make very significant impacts on the community that would not be possible if excessive taxes were applied without conditions. The 50% giving level of Giving Pledge members is in accordance with sustainability principles.

On a smaller scale, local giving clubs can also make a significant impact. For example, 100 Men on a Mission meets four times annually and each member gives $100 per meeting. The $10,000 generated per meeting is then given to a local charity. Giving clubs such as this can generate significant income for local charities without much cost to the members (see "How," 2014). This type of low-burden group should be adaptable to almost any community and any full-time employee who manages their money well.

Corporate giving The after-tax corporate profits for 2012 were about $1.5 trillion (see "US Corporate," 2014). Total corporate giving for 2012 was $18 billion, 6% of total giving (see "Giving," 2013). Individuals gave $229 billion in 2012, 13 times the corporate giving total. Corporation's total giving is only about 1% of their after-tax profits at a time when corporate profits are at their highest levels in 65 years (Norris, F., 2014). With over one million charitable organizations (see "Charitable," 2014), corporations should easily be able to find organizations that fit with their mission.

Investment Priorities for Community Sustainability

The following activities by individuals, businesses, churches, and community organizations will have high sustainability impact if enacted by large numbers of people:

Giving Increasing planned, prioritized, contemporary, and higher-percentage giving by those with excess resources, local giving clubs, and large giving organizations. Create an investment priority list: start by picking three to five high-impact areas where you want to make a difference and start investing in existing organizations. Existing organizations make the most efficient use of resources. If no organization exists for a specific impact area, the wealthy have the resources to start organizations.

Volunteerism Increasing targeted volunteerism to at least 50% in each community through local connections.

Preventative healthcare through volunteerism and businesses
- exercise incentives
- nutrition incentives
- vaccines research, development and use

Volunteering in healthcare and welfare
- long-term care for the elderly and disabled
- long-term care for the mentally ill
- community mentoring and Celebrate Recovery for those in recovery, rehabilitation, and homelessness
- establishment of comprehensive community shelters by neighborhood residents, businesses, churches, and other organizations.
- Family-to-family and peer-to-peer, long-term, comprehensive, mentoring
- voluntary use of internet blocking programs that filter addictive material

Volunteering or business initiatives in environmental sustainability
- adopting and promoting diets that replace beef with poultry, fish, or vegetables
- soil conservation
  - year-round cover crop programs
- community gardens that donate excess produce to those in need (eg. ampleharvest.org and www.cultivateiowa.org) and incorporate employment programs for suitable individuals in rehabilitation programs
- household consumption reduction, reuse, and recycling
- use of renewable energy and alternatives to fossil fuels

It is the lack of in-depth involvement by the majority of prosperous and skilled workers in our communities that has allowed unsustainable governmental practices to become entrenched. Communities were designed by God for every person to be involved with helping others. We would have sustainable communities and governments now if such interactions were common.

Chapter 7

Divine Love

The Superior Nature of Divine Love

Problems arise when we rely on limited resources. Fossil fuels are an excellent example. They are non-renewable and have never been the best long-term solution. Our short-term reliance on them is causing long-term problems. The sun, on the other hand, is a pollution-free, unlimited source of energy. Had the research and development funds invested in fossil fuels to date been invested in renewable energy, we almost certainly would have had affordable and reliable renewable energy by now given the pace of technological advancement in that time period. In addition, renewable energy is catching up with fossil fuels in spite of relatively limited overall investment. Fossil fuels were easier and cheaper to develop in the short-term, but harder to deal with in the long-term.

People are limited; God is not. Reliance on non-divine loves makes them into idols. Non-divine loves were never intended to be a foundation for our lives because of their innate limitations. When we make a non-divine love our life purpose or foundation, we make it an idol.

Creator's Role in Defining the Creation

Logically, it is not possible for anyone or anything other than our Creator to define us. The Creator defines the creation. A work of art is defined at some level by the artist or sculptor. In photography, the composition is defined by the photographer according to the intended meaning. For example, the interplay between light and clouds can convey dramatic outbursts or a sense of foreboding. However, the camera and the image are both incapable of defining the photographer. Likewise, they are powerless to do anything creative apart from the creator. As in this analogy, it is not possible for another human or possession to define us because they did not create us. When people define themselves with another human or possession, they are not in touch with the Creator-creation reality. They have created a false reality for themselves that is ultimately self-destructive. False realities are not sustainable because actual reality is not being addressed. The only way to build healthy, long-term relationships is to be defined by a healthy source of unconditional love. The Creator is the only pure and consistent source of unconditional love.

Why Must Divine Love Be First?

To prevent idolatry Given the consequences of idolatry, preventing it must be a priority. When we idolize human relationships, it weakens those relationships to the degree that the other person is idolized. Whenever we idolize another person, we end up demonizing them when they let us down. Relationship idols occur when we make another person the one who defines us. In our idolatry, we make them responsible for our neediness, attitudes, and feelings.

I had a pattern of idolizing and then demonizing friends. During college, I idolized and depended on my best friend. At the time, I was attending a church with legalistic tendencies, and my friend began to pull away from the legalistic behavior he saw in the church and in me. One weekend, his brother and a group of friends from out of town came to visit him. He completely excluded me from the events of that weekend and several other weekends. I was deeply hurt and almost ended our friendship. I was letting the rejection define me. Later, I was relieved that I didn't express an intent to end the relationship because the fruit of remaining in the friendship became so apparent. In fact, after recovering from the hurt, it became a turning point for me. It was the point when I learned to accept him for who he was. As a result, the friendship grew much stronger.

We can let people define us in small or large ways. Many claim to not make idols out of their relationships. They claim to have no fear or resentment in their relationships even though they express highly negative messages such as swearing and threats. Whenever there is fear driven by insecurity or resentment expressed in a relationship, it is due to idolatry. Fear and resentment always reveal an identity issue. The higher the degree of expression, the greater the identity issue. Everyone idolizes their relationships to some degree because everyone expresses some degree of fear and resentment. For example, no one loves their enemies perfectly or responds to offenses perfectly. God's standards are much higher than our standards. He considers all fear and resentment the result of idolatry.

Personally, I have struggled in this area, but God has also brought me much further than I used to be. I used to remain angry for extended periods. Now, God helps me let offenses go much faster by finding identity in Him. For example, if I felt betrayed by gossip, I let that define me and stayed angry with the person who gossiped. Now it is clear that I was hurting myself the most and that it was and is unhealthy for me to hold on to resentment. I can let things go on the basis of not damaging myself or my relationships, especially my relationship with God.

To free us from shame and striving   Nothing can free us more than unconditional acceptance. This is why divine love is the most important love. When we are accepted in spite of our selfishness, we no longer need to remain ashamed or worried. We don't have to do anything to be accepted because we are accepted unconditionally as long as we are in a relationship with God through Christ. Being fully accepted frees us from having to put on a front to get what we want, to look good, or to fit in. God's love naturally results in positive action from the recipients of His love. This is why people who have experienced God's healing after a painful divorce and abandonment by their married friends have a lower level of elitism. They befriend social outcasts because they have been outcasts themselves.

To free us from cultural faith   Cultural faith is faith practiced from and motivated by tradition and social norms. Cultural faith is based in selfishness. It asks, "What can I get from being involved in church," instead of, "What can I give?" The power to be authentic can only come from God. When we lose confidence in the ability of cultural standards to satisfy us and become confident in unconditional acceptance, we can move away from cultural faith and toward relational faith. Relational faith brings joy as a byproduct of the relationship.

Happiness as a Byproduct of a Healthy Relationship with God

We cannot be happy unless we have a healthy relationship with God. The beatitudes (Matthew 5: 3-12 GNB) describe specific aspects of personal recovery and "[happiness]" as a byproduct of a relationship with God.

"Happy are those who know they are spiritually poor. The Kingdom of Heaven belongs to them!" Knowing we are spiritually poor means knowing that we need a relationship with God. A relationship with God results in being with God in His kingdom. Relationships fill the "[poverty]" in our lives.

Happiness is a byproduct of the freedom of letting go and refocusing on God's goodness "Happy are those who mourn; God will comfort them!" A relationship with God allows us to process grief. When we tell God exactly what we are feeling in a way that values the relationship, He comforts us with His loving presence. This comfort allows us to forgive others. This letting go of resentment allows us to refocus on the goodness in our lives.

Happiness is a byproduct of humility "Happy are those who are humble; they will receive what God has promised!" If we are too reliant on ourselves, we block our relationships with God and others. Humility, however, allows us to receive help from God and others for all aspects of life. Humility also helps us forgive those who hurt us. His help relieves stress and that makes us happy as a byproduct.

Happiness is a byproduct of caregiving relationships "Happy are those whose greatest desire is to do what God requires. God will satisfy them fully." According to Micah 6:8, God "requires" mercy, justice, and humility. "He has shown you, O man, what is good; and what does the Lord require of you. But to do justly, to love mercy, and to walk humbly with your God." Mercy, justice, and humility are all key to relationships with God, others, and our communities. As people reach out to those in need, relationships are built between the care provider and the person in need and that, in turn, has an impact on others. Caregiving relationships, such as delivering meals to the homebound, mentoring those in prison, and providing community for the mentally ill, infuse mercy, justice, and humility into the wider community. God asks us to look after the outcasts and vulnerable people in our communities. I have been involved in community service as a volunteer for almost 15 years and have witnessed the effects of mercy, justice, and humility at every event.

Happiness is a byproduct of being merciful to others "Happy are those who are merciful to others; God will be merciful to them!" Showing mercy to others does two things in our lives: it reinforces our ability to be merciful to ourselves and it allows us to receive mercy from God. Alternatively, when we aren't merciful, we block mercy and grace from God. According to Mark 11:25, "And when you stand praying, if you hold anything against anyone, forgive them, so that your Father in Heaven may forgive you your sins."

Happiness is a byproduct of knowing who God is "Happy are the pure in heart. They will see God." Jesus is the only One who can purify our hearts, which can only occur if we are in relationship with Him. Through relationship, we come into His presence and see Him for who He really is. His presence makes us happy as a byproduct of knowing who He is.

Happiness is a byproduct of having peaceful relationships "Happy are those who work for peace; God will call them His children!" Again, "children" of God indicates the importance of having an actual relationship with God. Relationship with God is the driver for seeking peace with others. Peace with others makes us happy.

"Happy are those who are persecuted because they do what God requires. The kingdom of Heaven belongs to them!" If we do what God requires, we will be persecuted. We are to seek God's kingdom, not earthly kingdoms. God's work brings us joy as a byproduct even in the face of persecution. God requires us to do our part to work for peace by loving our enemies. This principle applies to the last beatitude as well.

"Happy are you when people insult you and persecute you and tell all kinds of evil lies against you because you are my followers. Be happy and glad for a great reward is kept for you in Heaven. This is how the prophets who lived before you were persecuted."

The "8 Principles" of Celebrate Recovery (Warren, R. et al. 2014) and the "Habits of Happiness" Philippians series, September 22-November 17, 2013, (Warren, R., 2013) both cover the principles of happiness. In-depth coverage of the 8 Principles is possible through a Celebrate Recovery step study.

Why Divine Love is Superior

Divine love is infinite

"And I pray that you, being rooted and established in love may have power, together with all the Lord's holy people, to grasp how wide and long and high and deep is the love of Christ and to know this love that surpasses knowledge-that you may be filled to the measure of all the fullness of God. Now to Him who is able to do immeasurably more than all we ask or imagine, according to His power that is at work within us, to Him be glory in the church and in Christ Jesus throughout all generations, for ever and ever! Amen." (Ephesians 3:17-21)

Divine love is unconditional In Ephesians 3:17-21, "high" indicates that divine love is superior in nature, and "wide and long" indicates that divine love is infinite. One aspect of its infinity is its dependability. We can count on God's love anywhere, any time. He comes through when we least expect it.

"Turn, Lord, and deliver me; save me because of your unfailing love." Unconditional love delivers us from our fears. (Psalm 6:4)

"But I trust in your unfailing love; my heart rejoices in your salvation." Unconditional love gives us a trust foundation. (Psalm 13:5)

"But the eyes of the Lord are on those who fear him, on those whose hope is in his unfailing love." Unconditional love gives us a source of lasting hope. (Psalm 33:18)

"Your constant love reaches the Heavens; your faithfulness touches the skies." Unconditional love is faithful to us even when we are faithless. (Psalm 57:10 GNB)

"Your constant love is better than life itself, and so I will praise you." Unconditional love gives us life. (Psalm 63:3 GNB)

"Let your constant love comfort me, as you have promised me, your servant." Unconditional love comforts and teaches us. (Psalm 119:76 GNB)

"Deal with your servant according to your love and teach me your decrees." Unconditional love comforts and teaches us. (Psalm 119:124)

God's demonstration of unconditional love Jesus demonstrated that God's love is unconditional through the completely selfless act of dying for our sins. Jesus demonstrated that the very nature of His love is selfless. Because He was perfect, He was completely undeserving of the punishment of the cross. Therefore, Jesus's sacrifice was done only for our behalf. Because Jesus took the punishment only for us, it was a completely selfless and unconditional act of love.

We cannot give anything to the person who created us because we received everything from Him (Romans 11: 35-36). We would not exist without our Creator. Every part of our existence, material and immaterial, depends on the Creator who started it all and holds it all together. God created everything for us in a long, careful, deliberate, elegant, and mysterious process including matter in all its forms, from simple to complex (subatomic particles, molecules, cells, tissues, organs, organisms, and ecosystems), history, emotions, language, purpose, beauty, and relationships. As Tim Keller has explained, we "Come to Him with nothing.... Everything is a gift." Tim Keller's Psalm 95, July 7, 2002, sermon podcast, Redeemer Presbyterian Church, explains this point well (Keller, T., 2002).

"Who has ever given to God that God should repay them. For from Him, through Him, and for Him are all things. To Him be the glory forever!" (Romans 11:35-36)

Divine love is complete Since no person is completely unselfish, we cannot love completely as God does. It is not possible for humans to love to the fullest extent or to complete another person. God is the sole possessor of complete love, and we are to find "immeasurably more" satisfaction in Him (Ephesians 3:19-20) than any other source of love. People will always disappoint us at some level.

"The church is Christ's body, the completion of him who himself completes all things everywhere." (Ephesians 1:23 GNB)

"And so we know on rely on the love God has for us. God is love. Whoever lives in love lives in God and God in them. This is how love is made complete among us." (1 John 4:16-17)

Divine love is everywhere   Unlike humans, with God, we can share anytime, anywhere. Ephesians 4:4-6, "One God and Father of all, who is over all and through all and in all," indicates that God is in total control because He is everywhere. In my life, there have been many times where God was the only one in the moment and in the place to provide guidance and help that no one else could.

"There is one body and one Spirit, just as you were called to one hope when you were called; one Lord, one faith, one baptism; one God and Father of all, who is over all and through all and in all." (Ephesians 4:4-6)

"Where can I go from your Spirit? Where can I flee from your presence? If I go up to the Heavens, you are there; if I make my bed in the depths, you are there. If I rise on the wings of the dawn, if I settle on the far side of the sea, even there your hand will guide me, your right hand will hold me fast. If I say, 'Surely the darkness will hide me and the light become night around me,' even the darkness will not be dark to you; the night will shine like the day, for darkness is as light to you." (Psalm 139:7-12)

Divine love is all-knowing   Only our Creator truly understands us. He understands us much better than we understand ourselves. He understands us much better than others understand us. He knows us fully and how to use our circumstances and relationships to help us grow and to strengthen us for the challenges of life.

God's love is the only love that prepares us for whatever comes
Any of us can have our individual world disrupted in a
moment or over time. We cannot control circumstances
and people; we can only control our response to them. This
is by design. God doesn't want us to rely on earthly
security or our own limited control over our lives. He
wants us to rely on Him so that we don't break down
when the unexpected does happen. He doesn't want us to
despair from a broken identity that relied on something
other than Him. He wants us to know that we are still
valuable to Him even if we lose our job or lose a spouse.
Authentic Christians are perhaps the only people in
recorded history to display genuine joy in circumstances of
losing everything, including their lives. Polycarp, second
century bishop of Smyrna, was executed at the age of 86.
As Polycarp spoke to his interrogators before his execution
"he was full of courage and joy. His face shone with
inward light…. The proconsul was astounded" (Arnold, E.,
The Early Christians). Betsie ten Boom, a Dutch prisoner of
war in Nazi Germany, displayed genuine joy in
Ravensbruck concentration camp and ministered to the
needs of fellow prisoners in spite of the fact that she was
dying. She maintained a positive attitude during her
imprisonment until her death (Ten Boom, C., *The Hiding
Place*). These believers were both sane and joyful as they
approached death in extreme circumstances.

Eternal protection   Culture can't provide the type of
protection we need. We need protection that covers all
circumstances and people. Only God can do that.
According to John 14:27, Jesus promised a different kind of
protection: "Peace I leave you… not as the world gives."
God does not give us cultural safety. He does not protect
us from circumstances and people. Instead, He gives us

His peace—eternal peace—and safety in the new creation inheritance. This is an imperishable material and spiritual inheritance.

Material safety and security on earth does not last, and we have little control over it. With an eternal, imperishable inheritance, it doesn't matter what happens to our material possessions as long as we have been good stewards of it. God does not hold us responsible for what is outside of our control. With an eternal inheritance, we can rest in God's control in spite of any circumstances (Colossians 1:17), knowing that He will eventually renew everything that is broken. The material realm will not pass into the new creation, but faith, hope, and love will (1 Corinthians 13:13). This is why storing up treasures on earth for personal security is irrelevant (Luke 12: 13-21).

"Peace I leave with you. My peace I give you. I do not give to you as the world gives. Do not let your hearts be troubled and do not be afraid." (John 14:27)

"He is before all things and in him all things hold together." (Colossians 1:17)

"I can do everything through Him who gives me strength." (Philippians 4:13)

"And God is able to make every grace overflow to you, so that in every way, always having everything you need, you may excel in every good work." (2 Corinthians 9:8 HCSB)

Divine love is intimate   Divine love is the combination of infinity ("immeasurably more," Ephesians 3:20) and intimacy. This is why it surpasses human love by an infinite margin. "High and deep" (Ephesians 3:18) indicates the intimate nature of God's love.

Why is God's love the most intimate love possible? Because it is indwelling (1 John 4:16-17). Indwelling intimacy is comprehensive because it enters into our heart, mind, and body. Humans cannot become part of us like God does. The indwelling Spirit is infinitely "high" (Ephesians 3:18) compared to human love.

"And so we know on rely on the love God has for us. God is love. Whoever lives in love lives in God and God in them. This is how love is made complete among us." (1 John 4:16-17)

Divine love is pure   Divine love is the only truly pure and perfect love. It is untainted by selfishness so that it can be given without any condition to all those who will receive it (John 1:12). 1 John 4:18 describes God's love as "perfect love."

Radical Nature of God's Love

As noted above, God's love is intended to prepare us for anything. A classic example of the radical nature of God's love is the story of God asking Abraham to sacrifice his son Isaac. God intentionally creates drama to strengthen our faith and to help us deal with our fears and insecurities (see Psalm 6:4 and Psalm 119:76 below). God looked bad in this story. Why would he ask Abraham to sacrifice Isaac, the son of a miraculous birth through which God's promises to Abraham were seemingly to be fulfilled? Abraham was obedient to God because, over the course of a lifetime, he had come to know God's character. In the end, God resolved the drama through Jesus. His request to Abraham was a prefiguring of what He would do with His Son, not Abraham's son. In essence, God was saying, "I'm not going to have you sacrifice your son, but I will sacrifice my Son." It turns out that Isaac was not the key to God's promise to Abraham that he would father a nation of innumerable descendants. Drama was needed to bring the point home. The story was about Jesus from start to finish (Romans 4). God's promise to Abraham concerned spiritual children, not physical descendants or a nation. God was talking about building His kingdom through the Messiah that would be one of Abraham's descendants. Jesus fulfilled the promise to Abraham through His death and resurrection. It was another indication of the radical nature of God's love (Romans 6:5). Only a Creator is capable of taking on Himself the sins of others and putting that sin to death in an infinite spiritual process of redemption.

The indwelling of the Spirit also indicates the radical nature of God's love, and being radically loved by God is exactly what we need. His unconditional love changes everything because it relieves us from trying to earn love through performance. According to 1 John 4:18, "There is no fear in love." Since "God is love," there is no fear in God when we relate to Him properly and understand who He is. We need the indwelling of God's spirit because true change only occurs from the inside out. "Perfect [divine] love drives out fear." The indwelling Spirit "drives out" fear because He is inside of believers. He can drive out character defects. We are not changed by ourselves or others from the outside in; we are changed by God from the inside out.

In summary, Jesus died for us, as one of us (Romans 6:5), and then came to live in us. The person who provided the greatest demonstration of love lives within believers in a way not possible for any other person. The Spirit indwells infinitely and intimately.

"God's plan is to make known his secret to His people, this rich and glorious secret which he has for all peoples. And the secret is that Christ is in you, which means that you will share in the glory of God." This is a promise about Heaven (the new creation). (Colossians 1:27 GNB)

"Set his seal of ownership on us, and put His Spirit in our hearts as a deposit, guaranteeing what is to come." The Spirit is the deposit guaranteeing the hope of Heaven. (2 Corinthians 1:22)

"For if we have been united with him in a death like His, we will certainly also be united with Him in a resurrection like His." (Romans 6:5)

The Type of Relationship God Wants with His People Always Reflects a Deep Desire for Intimacy

Husband and wife The indwelling Spirit is part of a spiritual marriage between God and His church. The type of relationship God wants with His church is like that of an intimate marriage. God does not describe His relationship with His people as a supervisory relationship. John 2: 1-12 describes Jesus's first miracle, turning water into wine at a wedding banquet. This story illustrated the type of intimacy God wants with His people. Tim Keller's "Lord of the Wine" sermon, November 17, 1996, explains this passage well (Keller, T., 1996).

"I am jealous for you with a godly jealousy. I promised you to one husband, to Christ, so that I might present you as a pure virgin to Him." (2 Corinthians 11:2)

"I saw the Holy City, the new Jerusalem, coming down out of Heaven from God, prepared as a bride beautifully dressed for her husband. And I heard a loud voice from the throne saying, 'Look! God's dwelling place is now among the people, and He will dwell with them. They will be His people and God Himself will be with them and be their God. He will wipe every tear from their eyes. There will be no more death' or mourning or crying or pain, for the old order of things has passed away...Come, I will show you the bride, the wife of the lamb.'" (Revelation 21:2-4, 9)

Father and children

"...the Spirit you received brought about your adoption to sonship. And by Him we cry 'Abba, Father.' The Spirit Himself testifies with our spirit that we are God's children." (Romans 8: 15-16)

"As a father has compassion on his children, so the Lord has compassion on those who fear him" (Psalm 103: 13)

"But when you pray, go into your room, close the door and pray to your Father, who is unseen." (Matthew 6:6)

Divine Love is the Foundation for Identity

Divine love is the only love that can completely deal with the formation of a healthy identity. None of us is capable of completely accepting ourselves as God does because our love and our understanding of ourselves are limited. One reason God accepts us as He created us is so that we can become better at accepting ourselves. People sometimes want us to be different from who we really are. If we try to live as someone we are not, we end up in an identity crisis.

What is the foundation for identity formation? Unconditional love is the only stable, long-term foundation for identity formation. By nature, another person cannot be a source of unconditional love. It must come from God. He demonstrated the unconditional nature of His love through creation and through Jesus. Ephesians 3:16-17 addresses identity formation; "inner being" indicates that identity is the target, and "rooted and established in love" indicates that identity is founded on unconditional love.

"I pray that out of his glorious riches He may strengthen you with power through his Spirit in your inner being, so that Christ may dwell in your hearts through faith. And I pray that you, being rooted and established in love, may have power, together with all the Lord's holy people, to grasp how wide and long and high and deep is the love of Christ." (Ephesians 3:16-18)

Why is God's love foundational? God's love is the one to "rely" on. We do need human love, but not as a foundation for our lives. We can identify ourselves only at a secondary level. This is good news. This means that our created identity is safe from our interference. Since people are not Creators, we don't have the ability to create or program our identities at the primary level. God defines us from the atoms up.

A foundation of divine love does not collapse in the storms of life like human love can. There are many examples of Christians experiencing joy in very severe circumstances.

———

Robert Murray M'Cheyne was a Scottish pastor in the 19th century. He had a serious heart condition and died at the age of 29. In spite of his continual struggle with poor health, he experienced consistent joy in his life because of his intimate relationship with God. During an illness, which he "had every reason to expect that [he] would soon be with [his] God," a friend attending to him noted "he felt that a single passage of the word of God was more truly food to his fainting soul than anything besides." His "spirit revived" and "eye glistened" when Psalm 41:1 was read to him, "Blessed is he that considereth the poor: the Lord will deliver him in time of trouble" (Bonar, A., *Memoir and Remains of Robert Murray M'Cheyne*).

What is the Process for Building an Identity Based on God's Love?

God has given us the process for becoming secure. It is learning to "rely" on His love. According to 1 John 4:16-17, love is made "complete" by "relying" on divine love as a foundation. Even Jesus chose to limit himself when He became incarnate (Hill, E., *The Trinity*). According to 1 John 4:17, "In this world we are like Jesus." Jesus depended on the Father (John 14:10, 31), and we are to follow His example and depend on Him (John 15:5), the Father, and the Holy Spirit. The pre-incarnate Jesus had no self-imposed limitations. He was coequal and coeternal with God.

"The words I say to you I do not speak on my own authority. Rather, it is the Father, living in me, who is doing His work... so that the world may learn that I love the Father and do exactly what my Father has commanded me." (John 14:10, 31)

201

Enter into a relationship with Him   God is relational by nature. This is most profoundly demonstrated in the Trinity. The Father, Son, and Holy Spirit coexist in perfect, eternal love (Hill, E., *The Trinity*). The Trinity is beyond any human's ability to fully grasp because the finite cannot fully grasp the infinite (Ephesians 3: 19-20). The significance for humans is to show us that God is relational by nature.

The implications of God being relational are game-changing because the vast majority of humans do not relate to God as if they can have a real relationship with Him. Unfortunately, most people have a cultural faith instead of a personal relationship with Him. Cultural faith keeps God at a distance and misses the whole point. Relationships have the greatest impact when a person realizes that they are fully known and accepted in spite of that knowledge. This is why a relationship with God is the most important relationship. Only He can know us completely and accept us completely in spite of our weaknesses.

God has built intentional mystery into His creation. He does not intend that we understand everything about Him (Isaiah 55:9). The purpose of mysteries beyond our comprehension is to cause us to seek and trust Him for what is beyond our control and to experience His relational nature. We all experience significant levels of mystery in relationships because everyone else's behavior is beyond our control. Why, then, should we object to mystery in our relationship with God? He places mystery in our relationship with Him so that we know that His nature is relational. He also gives us knowledge about Himself. We know enough about Him to understand that He is our Creator and Redeemer and, therefore, our most important relationship.

Receive His love 1 John 4:16 says, "And so we know and rely on the love God has for us." Here, John focuses on God's love for us and not our love for God because knowing our acceptance through God's unconditional love is the foundation of a healthy identity and a healthy life. First, God calls us to receive His love by entering into a relationship with Him (John 1:12; Romans 10:9). When we recognize His desire for relationship with us, we are called by God to accept His terms for the relationship: unconditional surrender to Him through faith in Jesus Christ. We acknowledge that we cannot defend ourselves on the basis of being good, we admit that we cannot pay for our sin and brokenness, and we accept our complete dependence on Jesus for entering into a relationship with God. The "Follow Me" teaching series from Saddleback Church, April 21-June 21, 2013, explains this process well (Laurie, G., et al., 2013).

Once a relationship with God has been established, the process of sanctification begins. Sanctification is the process of becoming more like Christ (Philippians 2:5; Ephesians 4:13-15, 24). It is designed by God to increase the amount of His unconditional love and decrease the amount of conditional love. Since God defines Himself as unconditional love (1 John 4:16), becoming more like Christ is to have higher degrees of unconditional love. Divine love recreates us by transforming our identity. The indwelling Spirit provides the transforming power and guidance to change.

"In your relationships with one another, have the same mindset as Christ Jesus... taking the very nature of a servant." (Philippians 2:5, 7)

"Until we all reach unity in the faith and in the knowledge of the Son of God and become mature, attaining to the whole measure of the fullness of Christ. Then we will no longer be infants, tossed back and forth by the waves, and blown here and there by every wind of teaching and by the cunning and craftiness of people in their deceitful scheming. Instead, speaking the truth in love, we will grow to become in every respect the mature body of Him who is the Head, that is, Christ." (Ephesians 4:13-15)

Why Do Most People not Prioritize Divine Love as the Most Important Love?

We default to the messages that are continually presented to us as standards. Every kind of media we encounter throughout the day has cultural messages defining standards of success. Pressure is generated by messages that reinforce the consequences of not adhering to the standard. Pressure is generated by knowledge of the large number of people pursuing cultural standards. If most people are pursuing a particular standard of success, we think that we will be unsuccessful if we don't pursue it too. The parable of the sower summarizes the issue.

"You, then, listen to the parable of the sower: When anyone hears the word about the kingdom and doesn't understand it, the evil one comes and snatches away what was sown in his heart. This is the one sown along the path. And the one sown on rocky ground — this is one who hears the word and immediately receives it with joy. Yet he has no root in himself, but is short-lived. When pressure or persecution comes because of the word, immediately he stumbles. Now the one sown among the thorns — this is one who

204

hears the word, but the worries of this age and the seduction of wealth choke the word, and it becomes unfruitful. But the one sown on the good ground — this is one who hears and understands the word, who does bear fruit and yields: some 100, some 60, some 30 times what was sown." (Matthew 13:18-23 HCSB)

People miss it (V19)   A lack of understanding prevents seeds of knowledge from growing. Without a starting point, the seed is lost.

Pressures of the world (V20-22)   Giving in to the pressure of cultural saturation leads to prioritizing cultural standards. One way or another, a lack of correct priorities leads to an unfruitful, unsustainable life.

Shallowness with God (V19-21)   People don't relate to God as a person and keep Him at a distance. Since they are closer to culture than God, they prioritize cultural standards.

Why Doesn't God Make Himself as Prominent as the Pressures of the World?

Relationships that work are never shallow or based on pressure, fame, wealth, or power. Relationships that work are based on unconditional love. Our closest relationships are those who accept us as we are and who care enough to help us get better. God approaches every relationship with gentleness and kindness. Kindness leads people to repentance, not pressure.

Chapter 8

The Gospel as the Basis for Serving

Why We Can't Settle for Cultural Standards

In different periods of throughout history, the Bible and Christians have come under attack. Radical scholars dismissed the historicity of the Bible only to be proven wrong by subsequent archaeological evidence. This has occurred up to recent times such as the finding of an inscription of the "House of David" (Kimberley, T., 2010). Cultural persecutions also continue up to the present in many parts of the world. Separation of church and state is needed to guard against manmade theocracies. The only theocracy that will work is the one Jesus will establish in the new creation. This will not happen in the present earth. The failure of manmade theocracies does not mean that faith has no role in society. It is clear that societies without faith struggle greatly such as the ones dominated by oppressive communist governments. Societies need the church to fulfill its intended role as salt and light to preserve and brighten society. The analogy of salt (Matthew 5: 13-16) suggests that God intended the church to play an important role in long-term community sustainability. The role of the church in leading community transformation by example and through the spectrum of truths found in the Gospel begins as people are transformed themselves (Swanson, E., and Williams, S., *To Transform a City*).

Many people establish good lives for themselves and their families in this prosperous nation and go no further. However, the good life is not necessarily the foundational life. All of us need a foundation on something that can't be taken from us and a connection with someone who knows us better than anyone else: our Creator. Any of us can lose everything we've worked for. Thus, life requires us to be prepared for whatever comes. Clearly, only God can provide the foundational relationship for life. Everything and everyone else can fail us. Fallible foundations such as job status and marital status can and do collapse. The divorce rates between 2000-2011 ranged from 3.5 to 4 divorces per 1,000 people compared to marriage rates of 6.8 to 8.2 per 1,000 people (see "National," 2013). The divorce rate remains high relative to the marriage rate. Divorce brings with it financial and relational difficulties. Over the years, I've heard people comment that they "lost all their friends" when they got divorced. In spite of all the commonly known evidence to the contrary, people continue to hope in marriage and career more than God.

It is not likely that everyone and everything will fail us, but everyone experiences significant loss at some point in life. A minority of people even make it to the end of life secure financially and relationally. Because the top performers get so much attention, the general population tends to put false hope in fantasies that somehow they will become one of those people who is financially secure rather than seeking a much more reliable and accessible form of security in God. The saturation of cultural success messages creates high levels of pressure. Pressure can create a panic that we won't survive in society if we go against cultural standards of success or cultural beliefs. As a result, giving in to cultural pressure to shoot for material and marital security is more appealing than living against this constant pressure. Marriage and career themselves are not bad but making them the sole life foundation is a self-destructive form of idolatry. We make it a foundational pursuit as a survival response to cultural pressure.

This life is only a very short beginning to the rest of eternity. Trusting in financial or marital security as a foundation is like settling for the first few years of a successful stock instead of choosing the long-term rewards. If someone chose to settle for the first year of growth in Apple stock when it took off, they would have missed out on most of the over 50-fold growth. What does it matter if someone "had it all" in a few years of earthly life only to lose it for all eternity? Sometimes success is God's most powerful judgment. If we don't want Him, He lets us settle for what we want to our utter destruction. The Accuser fools people into spending their entire lives trying to survive by meeting cultural standards. It is his most effective weapon.

Many successful people make the choice to reject God or keep Him at a distance in return for their earthly success. They want to protect their life from God fearing that He will ask them to change something or give up some of their success. He does ask us to stop engaging in behaviors that damage us and our relationships. He will ask us to stop sleeping around, looking at pornography, gambling, swearing, ignoring the needs of others, and putting our idols before Him.

However, what He gives in return is far better. He gives us life and peace now, often a better work-life balance, and then an eternity of success in an untainted realm.

Protecting what we have on earth now is no deal compared to eternity. Everything we do here is impacted by human brokenness. The most efficient and satisfying work possible doesn't begin until Heaven. People that reject God will miss out on this by their own choice. One day, they will realize that they traded eternity for a few very imperfect decades on earth and that everything gained in this life without Christ will be lost in the next life (Luke 9:23-25; 1 Corinthians 15:54). Earthly gains are negated without Christ.

What Can Christ Give Us That We Can't Get from the World?

Choosing to reject God is choosing to miss the most important relationship, the relationship with the One who knows us better than anyone else. God does not want us to settle for anything less than loving Him first. Personal sustainability is best facilitated by a relationship with our Creator. Relationships involve specific persons and specific relational terms. The persons of the Trinity take on specific roles and collaborate with each other in their relationship with us.

Our Creator defines the terms of our relationship with Him. When a craftsman makes a piece of furniture, He determines the raw materials, the shape, the size, the style, and the function. God defines Himself as Master and Lord and He defines our purpose according to how He created us. We don't define Him or instruct Him. The Designer knows what is best for us far better than we do. Our choices are often the opposite of what is best. It is astounding that we try to tell our Creator what to do, but we all do it. I was convinced that becoming a professor was the best life path for me. Academic teaching and research turned out to be far from best, and I burned out of both. God knew what was best far better than I did and opened the door to a much better fit in spite of me. This brought awareness of grace because it was so clear that I was given a second chance that I didn't deserve. My performance-oriented approach was the opposite of what was best and God gave me a second chance anyway. That got my attention and drew me to Him.

God's terms for relationship   God's requirement for relationship with Him is acceptance of His provision of Jesus for us. Jesus came to earth to be the mediator between God and people. An infinite, divine process of forgiveness took place in the death and resurrection of Jesus through His perfect sacrifice for sin. Our perfectly holy and infinite God took our sin upon Himself and was killed as part of a pre-determined, specific plan to redeem humans. This sacrifice was for us so that we could receive His Spirit into our heart, mind, and life. It is only God's presence inside us that makes us presentable to God. Otherwise, we would not be ready for a relationship with God. A relationship with God is not possible unless we are cleansed by Christ and conformed to His ways. Our forgiveness is complete when we accept His terms. God took our sin and asks for acceptance of His Son's sacrifice on our behalf and acceptance of His headship in our lives for the rest of life (Matthew 28:20). If we accept these terms, we begin a relationship with God.

Lordship   Acceptance of forgiveness is the easy part; acceptance of Christ's lordship in our lives is the hard part. Most people balk at giving God control of their lives because they think He will ask for sacrifices that will make them unhappy. God does ask us to live sacrificially as part of being in a relationship with Him as His children. However, it turns out that we are happier living a sacrificial life in a relationship with God than living for ourselves (Luke 9:23-25).

"Then he said to them all: 'Whoever wants to be my disciple must deny themselves and take up their cross daily and follow me. For whoever wants to save their life will lose it, but whoever loses their life for me will save it. What good is it for someone to gain the whole world, and yet lose or forfeit their very self?'" (Luke 9:23-25)

Once we enter into a relationship with God, He has a specific way for us to relate to Him. We come to Him on His terms alone to begin a relationship and then rely on His terms to grow in that relationship. This is why other paths to God fail. They try to relate to God on the wrong terms. God is a specific trio of persons, who have worked together to create a specific plan for all of creation and who have been involved with carrying out this plan throughout eternity. Unbiblical beliefs are not God's specific plan.

God wants the most intimate relationship with us as possible, a spiritual marriage in which His Spirit comes to live inside of us. This indwelling is the highest level of intimacy possible. He facilitates an ongoing relationship with Him through the indwelling Holy Spirit. God knows everything about us because He created us. He can teach us anything about ourselves or life that we need to know through the Spirit. We need Him to lead us in the details of life. God wants us to fully depend on Him. He wants to be our guide moment by moment. Without this in-the-moment guidance, we miss out on opportunities that only God can bring. This is important because God brings the best opportunities. God is our in-the-moment mentor. No one else can do that. Choosing cultural standards over God causes us to miss out on God-given opportunities and dehumanizes us by distancing and separating us from our Creator, the only One who can re-create us to be fully human.

The basis for sacrificial service The basis for a sacrificial life is all that God has done in history and in the present to redeem us and re-create us and what he will do in the new creation (Heaven). Those who have been redeemed are more aware of all God has done to save and sanctify them. Personally, I could not help but be thankful for a second chance that I didn't deserve after so many years of brokenness.

After God initiated a relationship with me in the fall of 2005, rapid and unexpected changes took place in my life. Within four months, some major areas of dysfunction had changed. Unfortunately, those were not the only areas that needed to change! It was clear that God's presence was changing my life for the better. By the end of a year of experiencing God's peace on a daily basis, it was clear that He wasn't going anywhere. I experienced many things for the first time during this period, including waking up in the morning without an alarm clock for assistance with gratefulness and joy, daily peace in spite of circumstances, less fear of cultural standards, and less need to figure things out. I used to worry constantly about the future, thinking that would somehow help me survive in the real world. The changes in my life made it clear that God knew better than I did how to run my life. After being suicidal for three years, I was simply happy to be alive. It was the first time I had truly felt alive without an absolute dependency on cultural standards for validation as a person.

This thankfulness lifted the weight of worry and made me want to know God more. Over the next four years, I spent significant amounts of time getting to know God better through the Bible and other books, prayer, and listening to teachings. I would often read alone at restaurants during this period, but I was not alone. I was in fellowship with God and learning from Him. I enjoyed it immensely. For me, it was clear that I didn't have life apart from God. It only made sense to put Him first in some difficult to decisions. I had to sacrifice some friendships that were not working. I had recovery issues that contributed to the demise of some relationships, but it didn't make sense to continue prioritizing relationships with people who didn't understand or believe the new relationship I had found with God. Some thought I was using God for my own gain. Nothing could have been further from my mind. I had been dead and had found life. Why would I not make that known? Even though sacrifice is difficult, life change makes sacrifice for God much more natural.

Eternal security in the new Heaven and the new earth is an even more compelling reason than life change to accept God's terms for a relationship. God will remake the present earth and repair the damage done to it by humans. God will do some of this Himself, and He will also use people to rebuild cities. This is the Heaven that believers will go to after they die. We will spend eternity with God in the new earth and will work with God in rebuilding ruined cities (Isaiah 61). We will be doing what we were made to do. Work will not be inhibited by broken relationships and inefficient technology. Thus, work will be fulfilling instead of frustrating.

The new creation will be so good that God expects us to sacrifice for His kingdom now in anticipation of what is to come. As discussed, a broken earth can't be the ultimate destination. Sacrifice is to be expected in a broken realm. It is a responsibility of being God's children and heirs (Romans 8:17). God expects His children to sacrifice because we are here only for a short time before entering into a perfect, eternal realm where the best work begins. He also knows that suffering provides opportunities to experience Him at deeper levels.

"Now if we are children, then we are heirs — heirs of God and co-heirs with Christ, if indeed we share in his sufferings in order that we may also share in his glory." (Romans 8:17)

Opportunities for Sacrifice

Probably the most frequent opportunity for sacrifice is in forgiving others quickly and unconditionally. People offend each other in small ways on a regular basis. God never intends us to hold on to these common offenses, and we self-destruct if we do. Our selfish nature automatically thinks in terms of returning offense for offense. The Lord's Prayer points the way forward for handling any offense. We are to forgive offenses on a daily basis as Christ forgave us (Ephesians 4:32).

"Our Father in Heaven,
hallowed be your name,
your kingdom come,
your will be done,
on earth as it is in Heaven.

Give us today our daily bread.
And forgive us our debts,
as we also have forgiven our debtors
And lead us not into temptation,
but deliver us from the evil one." (Matthew 6: 9-13)

"Be kind and compassionate to one another, forgiving each other, just as in Christ God forgave you." (Ephesians 4:32)

Other opportunities for sacrifice include giving when we are in need, giving when we receive nothing in return, and returning evil with good. All of these situations can apply to community mentoring as described previously throughout this book. We don't understand unconditional love until we experience it. When we experience it, we want to keep experiencing it. If we don't pass along God's unconditional love, we will find that we are creating blockages in our relationship with God (Matthew 6:14-15). We soon find that sacrificing His way is a lighter burden than not sacrificing (Matthew 11: 28-30).

The peace of unconditional acceptance is the best way to experience unconditional love. When we experience the fruit of unconditional love, joy, and peace, it changes our perspective. The disciples learned to rejoice in persecution (Acts 5: 41). Paul reached a high level of this victorious perspective (Philippians 3:10-11).

In spite of how much the disciples loved God, their emphasis was on God's love, not theirs. God's unconditional love forms the foundation for identity, and identity is the key personal component in all we think and do, the key to building sustainable communities, and the key to preserving a sustainable biosphere. We still have a chance at achieving a sustainable planet if we focus on personal sustainability first. Human behavior determines the outcome of every type of sustainability.

"We love because He first loved us. If anyone says, 'I love God,' yet hates his brother, he is a liar. For anyone who does not love his brother, whom he has seen, cannot love God, whom he has not seen. And He has given us this command: Whoever loves God must also love His brother." (1 John 4:19-21)

Epilogue

Over the next 30-40 years, trends in personal, economic, community, and environmental sustainability will interact and reinforce each other for better or worse. It may play out as a tug-of-war, with trends sometimes edging from one side of sustainability to the other. In the long-term, the Bible does not indicate that people will solve global problems. It indicates that we will not. However, it is in crisis that people can come to the end of themselves and then truly surrender to God. Unprecedented crisis is precisely what could bring about the great harvest mentioned in Revelation or a great harvest of any generation or era. This is in contrast to the time of Noah when there was no harvest. Christians have a great harvest in Christ to look forward to no matter what the times turn out to be. That provides foundational hope for the future in spite of what crises may occur.

Since God is the only One who can truly renew and re-create the earth as it was intended to be, the highest cause is not environmental or social justice to renew the earth in the present. But these are exactly the means by which we serve others in times of limited resources. By helping meet basic needs in times of crisis, we love our neighbor as they need to be loved. Environmental stewardship will become the main way to help the most people meet the basic needs of food and water. It is the lack of sufficient environmental stewardship on a global scale that has brought the world to the point where food and freshwater sustainability will be in question over the coming decades. If tipping points are crossed, soil and freshwater supplies will not be replenished in the short-term. Accordingly, all people can and should be involved in these environmental stewardship efforts.

Several sustainability trends are combining in countries throughout the world to create an environment and global community that will lack the resources to address basic needs if left unaddressed. All of the sustainability categories described in this book could grow to unsustainable levels.

In-depth, long-term service to others opens the door to sharing the Christian faith, a faith which brings lasting change to broken lives, broken communities, and broken nations. Environmental and social justice are means to do the kingdom building work of the church. Environmental and social justice may be losing causes in a long-term, society-wide, literal sense, but they are the practical means by which the church can serve the lost and introduce them to the Re-Creator, the eternal God, who will one day make all things right by renewing the Heavens and the earth. While we cannot ultimately hope in human efforts to bring about the physical renewal of the earth or international peace, we can experience abundant life and lasting hope in Christ in spite of whatever circumstances occur.

June 2014
Ames, Iowa

Bibliography

2013 Manufacturing Highlights. (n.d.). Retrieved May 2014, from
http://www.interfaceglobal.com/Sustainability/Our-Progress/AllMetrics.aspx

A Snapshot, Diabetes in the United States. (2014). Retrieved from
http://www.cdc.gov/media/DPK/2014/images/diabetes-report/Infographic1-web.pdf

About Christian Community Development Association. (n.d.). Retrieved June 2014, from
http://www.ccda.org/about

About Us. (n.d.). Retrieved July 21, 2014, from
http://www.celebraterecovery. com/site-map

Ackman, B. (2010, April 12). **Bill and Karen Ackman**. Retrieved , from http://givingpledge.org

Alexander, E. (2012) *Proof of Heaven: A Neuroscientist's Near-Death Experience and Journey into the Afterlife*. New York, N.Y.: Simon and Schuster

Allen, T. (2013, April 22). **Provision of deficit and debt data for 2012 - first notification**. Euro area and EU27 government deficit at 3.7% and 4.0% of GDP respectively. Retrieved from
http://epp.eurostat.ec.europa.eu/cache/ITY_PUBLIC/2-22042013-AP/EN/2-22042013-AP-EN.PDF

Amazon Overview. (n.d.). Retrieved May 2014, from
https://www.worldwildlife.org/places/amazon

Amazon: Medicines from nature. (n.d.). Retrieved July 31, 2014, from http://www.conservation.org/where/Pages/amazonia.aspx

Anthoff, D., Nicholls, R., Tol, R., & Vafeidis, A. (2006). **Global and regional exposure to large rises in sea level, a sensitivity analysis**. Retrieved from http://www.tyndall.ac.uk/content/global-and-regional-exposure-large-rises-sea-level-sensitivity-analysis-work-was-prepared-st

Aquion Energy. *Technology Review*, 117, 40.

Arnold, E. (1997). *The Early Christians in Their Own Words* (4th ed.). Farmington, PA: Plough Pub. House.

Atmospheric CO_2. (n.d.). Retrieved July 31, 2014, from http://co2now.org

Baker, J. (2007). *Life's Healing Choices: Freedom from Your Hurts, Hang-ups, and Habits*. New York: Howard Books.

Berkowitz, B. (2011, August 15). **Buffett higher tax call strikes a nerve**. *USA Today*.

Biello, D. **Greenhouse Goo**. *Scientific American*, 309, 56-61.

Bittle, S., & Johnson, J. (2008). *Where Does The Money Go?: Your Guided Tour to the Federal Budget Crisis*. New York: Collins.

Blackaby, H. T., & Blackaby, M. D. (2004). *What's So Spiritual About your Gifts*. Sisters, OR.: Multnomah Publishers.

Bonar, A. A. (1966). *Memoir and Remains of Robert Murray M'Cheyne*. London: Banner of Truth Trust.

Bradshaw, J. (2005). *Healing the Shame that Binds You* (Expanded and updated ed.). Deerfield Beach, Fla.: Health Communications.

Branch, T. *America in the King Years* book series:
- Branch, T. (1988). *Parting the Waters: America in the King Years, 1954-63*. New York: Simon and Schuster.
- Branch, T. (1998). *Pillar of Fire: America in the King Years, 1963-65*. New York, NY: Simon & Schuster.
- Branch, T. (2006). *At Canaan's Edge: America in the King Years, 1965-68*. New York: Simon & Schuster.

Brault, M. (2012, July). **Americans With Disabilities: 2010**. Retrieved from http://www.census.gov/prod/2012pubs/p70-131.pdf

Brown, B. (2012). *Daring greatly: How the courage to be vulnerable transforms the way we live, love, parent, and lead.* New York, NY: Gotham Books.

Bullis, K. **Tesla Motors**. *Technology Review*, 117, 30-31.

Cabrini-Green. (n.d.). Retrieved July 2014, from http://blackhistory.com/content/ 62103/cabrini-green

California Central Coast Groundfish Project. (n.d.). Retrieved May 2014, from http://www.nature.org/ourinitiatives/regions/northamerica/unitedstates /california/howwework/ central-coast-groundfish-project.xml

Capper, J., Berger, L., Brashears, M., & Jensen, H. **Animal Feed vs. Human Food: Challenges and Opportunities in Sustaining Animal Agriculture Toward 2050**. *CAST*, 1-16. Retrieved from http://www.academia.edu/4564150/Animal_Feed_vs._H uman_ Food_Challenges_and_Opportunities _in_Sustaining_Animal_Agriculture_Toward_2050

Carson, R. L. (1962). *Silent Spring*. Boston: Houghton Mifflin.

Celebrating 35 Years of Refugee Resettlement. (n.d.). Retrieved July 2014, from http://worldrelief.org/refugee-resettlement

Changing the Face of Energy. (n.d.). Retrieved July 2014, from http://www.bloomenergy.com/about/

Charitable Giving Statistics. (n.d.). Retrieved May 2014, from http://www.nptrust.org/philanthropic-resources/charitable-giving-statistics/

Climate Change Indicators in the United States. (n.d.). Retrieved May 2014, from http://www.epa.gov/climatechange/science/indicators/ ghg/global-ghg-emissions.html

Climate Change: How do we know? (n.d.). Retrieved June 2014, from http://climate.nasa.gov/evidence/

Cloud, H. (2013). *Boundaries for Leaders: Results, Relationships, and Being Ridiculously in Charge*. New York, N.Y.: Harper Collins Publishers.

Comstock, O., & Jarzomski, K. (2014, March 19). **LED bulb efficiency expected to continue improving as cost declines**. Retrieved from http://www.eia.gov/todayinenergy/detail.cfm?id=15471

Corbett, S., & Fikkert, B. (2012). *When helping hurts: How to alleviate poverty without hurting the poor-- and yourself.* Chicago, IL: Moody.

Cormack, D. (1997). *Killing Fields, Living Fields: An Unfinished Portrait of the Cambodian Church, the Church that Would Not Die.* England: OMF International.

Corn Background. (2014, July 15). Retrieved from http://www.ers.usda.gov/topics/crops/corn/background.aspx#.U9qZLBZD1Bw

Corn Overview. (n.d.). Retrieved May 2014, from http://www.ers.usda.gov/topics/crops/corn/.aspx#.U5m_SxaQlFI

Dods, M. (2006). *The City of God.* New York: Barnes & Noble.

Effective Tax Rates for Taxpayers with the Top 400 Adjusted Gross Income, 1992-2009. (2013, May 17). Retrieved from http://www.taxpolicycenter.org/taxfacts/displayafact.cfm?Docid=566

Ferrell, C. L. (2006). **The Abolitionist Movement**. Westport, Conn.: Greenwood Press.

Fiscal Year 2013 Annual Report Programs at a Glance. (n.d.). Retrieved May 2014, from **http://www.lpcs online.org/s/uploads/documents/fy13 _programs_at_a_glance.pdf**

Fischetti, M. **Storm of the Century: Every Two Years**. *Scientific American*, 308, 58-67.

Foley, J. (2014, October). **A five-step plan to feed the world. National Geographic Food Compilation Special Issue for Iowa Hunger Summit**, 5-28.

Frank, T. (2011, December 9). **States expand lucrative pensions to more jobs**. *USA Today*.

Frankl, R. (2013, May 11). **Three Reasons US Rich Don't Give More to Charity**. *CNBC*. Retrieved from http://www.cnbc.com/id/100543099

Frankl, V. E. (1984, 1962). *Man's Search for Meaning* (Rev. and enl. ed.). Boston, Mass.: Washington Square Press.

Fraser, B. **Drying Rain Forest**. *Scientific American*, 308, 16.

Frequently Asked Questions. (n.d.). Retrieved May 2014, from http://givingpledge.org/faq.aspx

Freunberg, D. (2005). **Oral Lee Brown**. Retrieved from http://www.humanmedia.org/catalog/program.php?products_id=237

Gardeners. (n.d.). Retrieved December 19, 2014, from http://www.ampleharvest.org

Gipple, E., & Gose, B. (2012, August 19). **America's Generosity Divide. The Chronicle of Philanthropy**. Retrieved from http://philanthropy.com/article/America-s-Generosity-Divide/133775/

Giving to Empower Hardworking People. (n.d.). Retrieved May 2014, from http://www.worldvisionmicro.org

Giving USA: Charitable Donations Grew in 2012, but Slowly, Like the Economy (2013, June 18). The Chronicle of Philanthropy. Retrieved from http://www.philanthropy.iupui.edu/news/article/giving-usa-2013

Gladwell, M. (2008). *Outliers: The Story of Success.* New York: Little, Brown and Co.

Gladwell, M. (2009). *What the Dog Saw and Other Adventures.* New York: Little, Brown and Company.

Goleman, D. (1995). *Emotional intelligence.* New York: Bantam Books.

Goodland, R., & Anhang, J. (2009, November). **Livestock and Climate Change**, World Watch Report, November/December. Retrieved from http://www.world watch.org/files/pdf/Livestock% 20and%20Climate%20Change.pdf

Goodwin, D. K. (2005). *Team of Rivals: The Political Genius of Abraham Lincoln.* New York: Simon & Schuster.

Gore, A. (1994). **Introduction**. *Silent Spring* (1962). New York, N.Y.: Houghton Mifflin.

Gose, B., Frostenson, S., & López-Rivera, M. (2013, July 14). **10 Companies That Gave the Most Cash in 2012**. The Chronicle of Philanthropy. Retrieved from http://philanthropy.com/article/10-Companies-That-Gave-the/140261/

Guerin, O. (2011, January 28). **Pakistan floods still claiming lives, six months on. BBC News**. Retrieved from http://www.bbc.co.uk/news/world-south-asia-12308913

Guide for Industrial Waste Management. (n.d.). Retrieved May 2014, from http://www.epa.gov/epawaste/nonhaz/industrial/guide/

Hatfield, J., & Smith, D. (2014). **Food and agricultural waste: Sources of carbon for ethanol production**. *Carbon Management*, 4(2), 203-213. Retrieved from http://www.tandfonline.com/toc/tcmt20/4/2#.VJNN9can2gQ

Heathcote, A., Filstrup, C., and Downing, J. **Watershed Sediment Losses to Lakes Accelerating Despite Agricultural Soil Conservation Efforts**. *PLoS ONE*, 8: e53554. doi:10.1371/journal.pone.0053554 (2013).

Helman, C. (2014, April 15). **What America's 15 Most Profitable Companies Pay In Taxes**. *Forbes*. Retrieved from http://www.forbes.com/sites/christopherhelman/2014/04/15/what-americas-most-profitable-companies-pay-in-taxes/

Hill, E. (1991). *The Trinity*. Brooklyn, N.Y.: New City Press.

History of Federal Individual Income Bottom and Top Bracket Rates. (n.d.). Retrieved May 2014, from http://www.ntu.org/tax-basics/history-of-federal-individual-1.html

Horowitz, J., Ebel, R., & Ueda, K. (2010, November). **"No-Till" Farming Is a Growing Practice**. Retrieved from http://www.ers.usda.gov/publications/eib-economic-information-bulletin/eib70.aspx#.U8kUBhZD1Bw

Hourihan, M. (2014, April). **Historical Trends in Federal R & D.** Retrieved from http://www.aaas.org/sites/default/files/15pch02.pdf

Housing First. (n.d.). Retrieved December 17, 2014, from http://www.endhomelessness.org/pages/housing_first

How 100+ Men on a Mission Works. (n.d.). Retrieved May 2014, from http://100menonamission.com/how.html

Howe, D. W. (2007). *What Hath God Wrought: The Transformation of America, 1815-1848.* New York: Oxford University Press.

Hurricane Katrina pushed landfill business into overdrive. (2011, March 23). Retrieved from http://www.nola.com/katrina/index.ssf/2011/03/hurric ane_katrina _pushed_landf.html

Ideas to Change the World. (n.d.). Retrieved July 2014, from http://terrapower.com/pages/benefits

Illinois Drowning in Debt. (2014, January 7). Retrieved from http://www.illinoispolicy.org/illinois-drowning-in-debt-127-billion-and-counting/

Inman, M. **The true Cost of Fossil Fuels.** *Scientific American*, 308, 58-61.

Iowa Disaster History. (n.d.) Retrieved April 2014, from http://homelandsecurity.iowa.gov/disasters/iowa_disast er_history.html

Iowa Soils. (n.d.). Retrieved July 31, 2014, from http://www.iptv.org/iowapathways/mypath.cfm?ounid=ob_000144

Jones, J. (2014, January 8). **Record-High 42% of Americans Identify as Independents**. Retrieved from http://www.gallup.com/poll/166763/record-high-americans-identify-independents.aspx

Kaimowitz, D., Mertens, B., Wunder, S., and Pacheco, P. (2004). **Hamburger Connection Fuels Amazon Destruction**. Retrieved from http://www.cifor.cgiar.org/publications/pdf_files/media/Amazon.pdf)

Keller, T. **A Study of Ephesians: Who Is the Church?** Sermon on January 8, 2012, Redeemer Presbyterian Church Retrieved from http://www.gospelinlife.com/a-study-of-ephesians-who-is-the-church.html.

Keller, T. (1996, November 17). **Lord of the Wine**. Retrieved from http://sermons2.redeemer.com/sermons/lord-wine

Keller, T. (2002, July 7). **Worship**. Retrieved from http://sermons2.redeemer.com /sermons/worship

Keller, T. J. (2010). *Generous Justice: How God's Grace Makes Us Just*. New York, N.Y.: Dutton, Penguin Group USA.

Keller, T. J., & Alsdorf, K. L. (2012). *Every Good Endeavor: Connecting Your Work to God's Work*. New York: Dutton.

Keller, T. J., & Keller, K. (2011). *The Meaning of Marriage: Facing the Complexities of Commitment with the Wisdom of God*. New York: Dutton.

Kenny, P. **The Food Addiction**. *Scientific American*, 309, 44-49.

Kimberley, T. (2010, September 29). **Top Ten Biblical Discoveries in Archaeology**. Retrieved from http://www.reclaimingthemind.org/blog/2010/09/top-ten-biblical-discoveries-in-archaeology-2-house-of-david/

Klein, D. **The Introduction, Increase, and Crash of Reindeer on St. Matthew Island**. *J. Wildlife Management* 32, 350-367 (1968). J. Wildlife Management, 32, 350-367.

LaMonica, M. (2014, May 5). **Ambri Funding Influx Suggests a New Day for Grid Batteries**. *MIT Technology Review*. Retrieved from http://www.technologyreview.com/news/527061/ambri-funding-influx-suggests-a-new-day-for-grid-batteries/

LaMonica, M. **Cree**. *Technology Review*, 117, 36.

Landsat Top 10: International Deforestation Patterns in Tropical Rainforests. (2012, July 23). Retrieved from http://www.nasa.gov/mission_pages/landsat /news/40th-top10-amazon.html#.U5m8dRaQlFI

Laurie, G., Chan, F., Jesus, W. D., Moore, R., White, J., Noble, P., et al. (2013, April 21). **Follow Me**. Retrieved from http://www.saddlebackresources.com /024900_Follow-Me-What-It-Means-To-Be-A-Disciple-Of-Jesus-C3377.aspx

LeTourneau, R. G. (1972). *Mover of Men and Mountains: The Autobiography of R. G. LeTourneau*. (Moody Press ed.). Chicago: Moody Press.

Lew, M. (2010, May 15). **The World's Biggest Burgers**. Huffington Post. Retrieved from http://www.huffingtonpost.com/Menuism/the-worlds-biggest-burgers_b_1413536.html#s967541&title=1_Bobs_BBQ

Lewis, C. S. (1960). *The Four Loves*. New York: Harcourt, Brace.

Lopez, K. (2008, January 14). **Katrina volunteers come to stay**. *USA Today*.

Making the healthy choice the easy choice on school lunch trays. (n.d.). Retrieved December 19, 2014, from http://www.blankfoundation.org/impact/stories

Malaria Strategy Overview. (n.d.). Retrieved December 19, 2014, from http://www.gatesfoundation.org/What-We-Do/Global-Health/Malaria

Mann, M. **False Hope**. *Scientific American*, 310, 78-81.

Matthews, C. (2006, November 29). **Livestock a major threat to environment**. Retrieved from http://www.fao.org/newsroom/en/News/2006/1000448/index.html

Maxwell, J. (2014). **The Maxwell Plan**. Retrieved from www.maxwellplan.com

Maxwell, J. (2003). *Thinking for a Change: 11 Ways Highly Successful People Approach Life and Work*. New York: Warner Books.

McGranahan, G., Balk, D., & Anderson, B. **The Rising Tide: Assessing the Risks of Climate Change and Human**

Settlements in Low Elevation Coastal Zones. Environment and Urbanization, 19, 17-37.

McKibben, B. (2012, April 5). **Payola for the Most Profitable Corporations in History.** Huffington Post. Retrieved from http://www.huffingtonpost.com/bill-mckibben/big-oil-subsidies_b_1405499.html

McMillan, T. (2014, October). **The New Face of Hunger.** *National Geographic* Food Compilation Special Issue Provided for the Iowa Hunger Summit, 5-28

Meadows, D. H., & Randers, J. (2004). *The Limits to Growth: the 30-year update.* White River Junction, Vt: Chelsea Green Pub. Co.

Mercury. (n.d.). Retrieved May 2014, from http://www.oeconline.org/our-work/healthier-lives/pollutioninpeople/ report/chapter2/

Metaxas, E. (2007). *Amazing Grace: William Wilberforce and the Heroic Campaign to End Slavery.* New York, NY: Harper San Francisco.

Metaxas, E. (2013). *Seven Men: and the Secret of their Greatness.* Nashville: Thomas Nelson.

Metaxas, E. (2013, September 26). **Revive the Church, Revive the Culture**. *BreakPoint Commentaries*. Retrieved from https://www.breakpoint.org/bpcommentaries/breakpoint-commentaries-archive/entry/13/23420

Microfinance A Long-Term Solution to Poverty. (n.d.). Retrieved May 2014, from http://worldrelief.org/microfinance

Min, S., Zhang, X., Zwiers, F., & Hegerl, G. **Human contribution to more-intense precipitation extremes**. *Nature*, 470, 378-381.

Montgomery, D. (2012). *Dirt: The Erosion of Civilizations*. Berkeley: University of California Press.

Mooney, C. **The Truth About Fracking**. *Scientific American*, 305, 80-85.

Mundel, T., Elias, C., Golston, A., & Suzman, M. (2014). **What We Do**. Retrieved from http://www.gatesfoundation.org/What-We-Do

Municipal Solid Waste. (n.d.). Retrieved May 2014, from http://www.epa.gov/waste/nonhaz/municipal/

National Climate Assessment Report. (2014). Retrieved from http://nca2014.globalchange.gov/report

National Marriage and Divorce Rate Trends. (2013, February 19). Retrieved from http://www.cdc.gov/nchs/nvss/marriage_divorce_tables.htm

Nazi Euthanasia Program: Persecution of the Mentally & Physically Disabled. (n.d.). Retrieved May 2014, from http://www.jewishvirtuallibrary.org/jsource/Holocaust/disabled.html

Nepstad, D., McGrath, D., Alencar, A., Barros, A., Carvalho, G., Santilli, M., et al. **Frontier Goverance in Amazonia**. *Science*, 295, 629-631.

Neuman, S. (2014, January 20). **Oxfam: World's Richest 1 Percent Control Half of Global Wealth**. NPR. Retrieved from http://www.npr.org/blogs/thetwo-way/2014/01/20/264241052/oxfam-worlds-richest-1-percent-control-half-of-global-wealth

Norris, F. (2014, April 4). **Corporate Profits Grow and Wages Slide**. The New York Times. Retrieved from http://www.nytimes.com/2014/04/05/business/economy/corporate-profits-grow-ever-larger-as-slice-of-economy-as-wages-slide.html?_r=1

NRCS Cover Crop Termination Guidelines. (2013, June). Retrieved from http://www.nrcs.usda.gov/Internet/FSE_DOCUMENTS/stelprdb1167871.pdf

Obesity and overweight. (2014, May). Retrieved from http://www.who.int/mediacentre /factsheets/fs311/en/.

Ortberg, J. (2014). *Soul Keeping*. Grand Rapids, Mich.: Zondervan.

Our Services. (n.d.). Retrieved May 2014, from http://www.willowcreekcarecenter.org/about-us/our-services/

Owen, J. (1996). *The Mortification of Sin*. Fearn: Christian Focus.

Pall, P., Aina, T., Stone, D., Stott, P., Nozawa, T., Hilberts, A., et al. **Anthropogenic greenhouse gas contribution to flood risk in England and Wales in autumn 2000**. *Nature*, 470, 382-385.

Patton, M. (2012, June 20). **Gold, The Dollar, And Exploding Debt And Deficits**. *Forbes*.

Percent of Farmland Planted as Corn & Soybeans. (2004). Retrieved from http://www.extension.iastate.edu/Documents/soils/crop maps/pctc_s.pdf

Pledger Profiles. (n.d.). Retrieved May 2014, from http://givingpledge.org

Pomerleau, K. (2013, December 18). **Summary of Latest Federal Income Tax Data**. Retrieved from http://taxfoundation.org/article/summary-latest-federal-income-tax-data

Poore, R., Williams, R., & Tracey, C. (2000). **Sea Level and Climate**. Retrieved from http://pubs.usgs.gov/fs/fs2-00/

Pornography. (n.d.). Retrieved June 2014, from https://wsr.byu.edu/pornographystats

Randers, J. (2012). *2052: A Global Forecast for the Next Forty Years*. White River Junction, VT.: Chelsea Green Pub.

Rath, T. (2007). *Strengths Finder 2.0*. New York: Gallup Press.

Rationing and Recycling. (n.d.). Retrieved June 2014, from http://www.nationalww2 museum .org/learn/education/for-students/ww2-history/america-goes-to-war.html

Reich, R. B. (2010). *Aftershock: The Next Economy and America's Future*. New York: Alfred A. Knopf.

Rice, D. (2013, January 25). **Hurricane Sandy, drought cost U.S. $100 billion**. *USA Today*.

Rotman, D. (2014). **Technology and Inequality**. *Technology Review*, 117(6), 52-60

Rotman, M. (n.d.). **Lake Erie**. Retrieved May 2014, from http://clevelandhistorical.org/items/show/58#.U8p9sxZ D1Bx

Royte, E. (2005). *Garbage Land: On The Secret Trail of Trash*. New York: Little, Brown.

Rushe, D. (2013, October 22). **US CEOs break pay record as top 10 earners take home at least $100m each**. The Guardian. Retrieved from http://www.theguardian.com/ business/2013/oct/22/top-earning-ceos-100m-paychecks-record

Schlosser, E. (2001). *Fast Food Nation: The Dark Side of the All-American Meal*. Boston: Houghton Mifflin.

Shaw, A. (2013, July 4). **Joey Chestnut Wins 2013 Hot Dog Eating Contest – Again**. ABC News. Retrieved from http://abcnews.go.com/blogs/headlines/2013/07/joey-chestnut-wins-2013-hot-dog-eating-contest-again/

Singh, A. (2005). *One Planet, Many People: Atlas of Our Changing Environment*. Nairobi, Kenya: UNEP.

SNAP: Created to Answer the Question: How can protecting nature help ensure food, energy, water, and security for 9 billion or more people? (2013, September 24). Retrieved from http://www.nature.org/newsfeatures/pressreleases/scie nce-for-nature-and-people-snap-created.xml

Soares-Filho, B. S., Nepstad, D. C., Curran, L., Cerqueira, G. C., Garcia, R. A., Ramos, C. A., et al. **Modeling conservation in the Amazon basin**. *Nature*, 440, 520-523.

Stark, R. (2011). *The Triumph of Christianity: How the Jesus Movement Became the World's Largest Religion*. New York: HarperOne.

Stewart, J. (2013, July 19). **Richer Farmers, Bigger Subsidies.** New York Times. Retrieved from http://www.nytimes.com/2013/07/20/business/richer-farmers-bigger-subsidies.html?pagewanted=all&_r=0

Supportive Housing. (n.d.). Retrieved July 2014, from http://www.desc.org/housing.html

Swanson, E., & Williams, S. (2010). *To transform a city: Whole church, whole Gospel, whole city*. Grand Rapids, Mich.: Zondervan.

Talbot, D. (2014). **China's GMO Stockpile**. *Technology Review*, 117(6), 36-42.

Tanner, M. (2012, April 11). **The American Welfare State. How We Spend Nearly $1 Trillion a Year Fighting Poverty — and Fail.** Retrieved from http://www.cato.org/sites/cato.org/files/pubs/pdf/PA694.pdf

Taubes, G. **Which One Will Make You Fat?** *Scientific American*, 309, 60-65.

Ten Boom, C., & Sherrill, J. L. (1976, 1971). *The Hiding Place*. London: Hodder and Stoughton and Christian Literature Crusade.

The Numbers Count: Mental Disorders in America. (n.d.). Retrieved May 2014, from http://www.nimh.nih.gov/health/publications/the-numbers-count-mental-disorders-in-america/index.shtml

The PEACE Plan. (n.d.). Statistics originally retrieved May 2014, from http://saddleback.com/connect/ministry/the-PEACE-plan/lake-forest

United States Government Debt to GDP. (n.d.). Trading Economics. Retrieved May 2014, from http://www.tradingeconomics.com/united-states/government-debt-to-gdp

US Corporate Profits After Tax: 1.907T USD for Q1 2014. (n.d.). Retrieved May 2014, from http://ycharts.com/indicators/corporate_profits

US Welfare System - Help for US Citizens. (n.d.). Retrieved May 2014, from http://www.welfareinfo.org

USDA ERS database (n.d.). Retrieved October 10, 2014, from http://www.ers.usda.gov/data-products/feed-grains-database

Vergano, D. W. (2013, May 1). **When rain, rain won't go away**. *USA Today*.

Warren, J. K. (2006). *Evaporites: Sediments, Resources, and Hydrocarbons*. Berlin: Springer.

Warren, R. (2012). *The Purpose Driven Life: What on Earth Am I Here For?* (Expanded ed.). Grand Rapids, Mich.: Zondervan.

Warren, R. (2013, December 28). **Preparing for Transformation**. Retrieved from http://saddleback.com/watch/media/series/2129/preparing-for-transformation

Warren, R. (2013, September 22). **Habits of Happiness**. Retrieved from http://saddleback.com/watch/media/series/2067/The-Habits-of-Happiness

Warren, R., Amen, D., & Hyman, M. (2013). *The Daniel Plan: 40 Days To A Healthier Life* (International trade paper ed.). Grand Rapids, Michigan: Zondervan.

Warren, R., Holladay, T., Fields, D., Owens, B., & Warren, K. (n.d.). **Life's Healing Choices-The Beatitudes**. Retrieved July 21, 2014, from http://www.saddlebackresources.com/021500_Lifes-Healing-Choices-The-Beatitudes-C807.aspx

Warren, R. (2014, September 7). **Making the Most of Opportunities**. Retrieved from http://saddleback.com/watch/media/making-the-most-of-opportunities

Watts, J. (2012, June 7). **Amazon deforestation at record low**. *The Guardian*.

Weise, E. (2012, December 21). **EPA rules target mercury pollution, toxics from power plants**. *USA Today*. Retrieved from http://usatoday30.usatoday.com/money/industries/energy/story/2011-12-19/power-plants-mercury-rule/52142516/1

Where Your Federal Tax Dollars Go. (2014, April 14). *USA Today*.

Who Doesn't Pay Federal Taxes. (n.d.). Retrieved May 2014, from http://www.taxpolicycenter.org/taxtopics/federal-taxes-households.cfm

Wiles, R. (2012, April 22). **Pro athletes often fumble the financial ball.** *USA Today*. Retrieved from http://usatoday30.usatoday.com/sports/story/2012-04-22/Pro-athletes-and-financial-trouble/54465664/1

Williams, R. (2008, January 14). **Effective Tax Rates for Different Kinds of Households**. Retrieved from http://www.taxpolicycenter.org/UploadedPDF/1001122_effective_tax_rates.pdf

Wolf, R. (2012, January 9). **U.S. debt is now equal to economy**. *USA Today*.

Wolkowski, R., & Lowery, B. (2008). **Soil Compaction: Causes, Concerns, and Cures. UW Extension**. Retrieved from http://www.soils.wisc.edu/extension/pubs/A3367.pdf

World Corn Trade. (n.d.). Retrieved July 31, 2014, from http://www.ers.usda.gov/topics/crops/corn/trade.aspx#world

Worstall, T. (2013, July 3). **US Corporations Only Paid 13% Of Their Profits In Federal Tax: Apple Is The Explanation For This**. *Forbes*. Retrieved from http://www.forbes.com/sites/timworstall/2013/07/03/us-corporations-only-paid-13-of-their-profits-in-federal-tax-apple-is-the-explanation-for-this/

Wright, N. T. (2008). *Surprised by Hope: Rethinking Heaven, the Resurrection, and the Mission of the Church*. New York: HarperOne.

Wright, N. T. (2010). *After You Believe: Why Christian Character Matters*. New York, NY: HarperOne.

Young, S. (2012). *Jesus Today: Experience Hope Through His Presence*. Nashville: Thomas Nelson.

Ziegler, T. et al., (2013, May 7). 20 **Companies that Made the Most**. *CNN*.
http://money.cnn.com/gallery/news/companies/2013/05/06/500-most-profitable.fortune/20.html

Zweibel, K., Mason, J., & Fthenakis, V. **A Solar Grand Plan**. *Scientific American*, 298, 64-73.

The Story of JETT

JETT is dedicated to community service as a means of sustainability. Over time, JETT came together from lessons learned from each stage of life. When I arrived at Iowa State University in August of 1984, one of the first things I noticed was the scripture quote on the Parks library from John 8:32; "And ye shall know the truth, and the truth shall make you free."

Previously, I grew up Catholic and went to a Catholic primary school where I was a trouble maker. I was frequently in the principal's office and I ended up with several detentions. My least favorite class in primary school was religion. I had not made it a habit to read the Bible for myself at that time because I wasn't interested in Bible study. I became more interested as crisis came to our family in 8th grade and my best friends family began reaching out to me with their Christian faith. By the time I entered college, I was primed for making a stronger faith commitment. When I saw the quote from John 8:32, it stunned me. I knew that I wanted to be free from brokenness and insecurity and that quote indicated that God was probably the best source of freedom.

At that time, I understood little about recovery principles even though our family had been through counseling for a couple of years before my parents divorced. My 20s and 30s passed without a significant breakthrough in the freedom that John 8:32 described even though I longed for it. After almost ten years of a progressive career crisis and subsequent renewal transition in my late 30s, the breakthrough came. God made Himself known to me as a God of infinite, unconditional love and peace. I knew that He was trustworthy and would lead me through the good and bad times in the future. Up to that point, I had constantly worried about the future.

I only mentioned part of John 8:32. It turns out that the rest of the verse is empowered by the relational element of faith. When we know who God is, we want to honor him even in the difficult times. Life is hard for everyone and eventually it will reveal us and our beliefs. If we know who God is and have a relationship with Him, we will still honor Him and His ways when our world falls apart. If we don't know Him relationally, we boot and/or blame God when trouble comes. This pattern is indicated by the first part of John 8:32 "If you hold to my teaching, you are really my disciples."

My faith journey led to a relationship with the Creator that is there at all times. Relational faith led me to begin a new journey in personal sustainability through recovery, a journey that will take the rest of life. Community sustainability was added to the journey when I began volunteering at Lincoln Park homeless shelter in Chicago. It was the highlight of my week during an extended period of darkness.

Environmental sustainability was an interest as far back as primary school when we vacationed at many national parks and it helped lead to the decision to major in ecology in college. At Iowa State, I listened to sustainability lectures by department professors, Norman Myers, Paul Ehrlich, and others. Of particular concern was the news of the destruction of tropical rainforests for agriculture and subsequent abandonment of fields when the poor forest soils no longer produced sufficient yields.

Financial sustainability came to the forefront when the Republicans came to power in the presidency and both houses of congress and the national debt became much worse than ever before. I had anticipated a positive impact on national finances and was greatly disappointed. When it became apparent that our political leaders are not going to address our growing sustainability issues, I knew that people had to begin making a difference. That conviction grew until it was strong enough to get me over the hump of leaving a secure government job to start JETT.

John 8:32 is about sustainable faith manifested in sustainable living. Sustainable faith is constant through any circumstance in spite of our weaknesses and failings. Even if we are faithless at times, God is faithful and keeps His promises. Thus, it is fitting that a personal sustainability verse should form an acronym for a sustainability business called JETT.

JETT Services and Products

50/25 is JETT's common agenda for sustainability networking.

- **50:** Helping others helps us. Long-term sustainability is possible when at least 50% of US population act in a *provider* role involved in helping under-resourced (personally, financially or other areas of health), underskilled (lacking training) people according to sustainability priorities.
- **25:** At least 25% of the US population involved in identity-based recovery programs that address health holistically.

Who should join the 50/25 sustainability network

Collectively, people and organizations that join the 50/25 sustainability network can help people in need in all 7 areas of health according to their personal or organizational expertise.

- o Leaders or leading agencies in the 7 areas of health (Spiritual, Relational, Emotional, Mental, Physical, Financial, Vocational)
- o **How does the 50/25 sustainability network work:** In order for people to change lifelong habits, they need repetition of the right messages and they need to hear it from a variety of trusted organizations. A network of organizations helps people and communities change more than any one organization. A network that is too small won't provide sufficient repetition from a wide enough variety of sources to initiate life change.
- o JETT utilizes client exchange to facilitate client growth. JETT refers clients to provider

organizations according to client need and provider organization expertise. JETT has contacts in all 7 areas of health.

What are the sustainability priorities needed for a viable sustainability movement?
1. Personal health
2. Community health
3. Vocational health
4. Environmental health

JETT Sustainability Coaching and Speaking Services

JETT can help you or your organization adjust your existing vision and goals to impact sustainability. Through speaking and group coaching, JETT can:
- Increase personal and group awareness of how to make a sustainability impact.
- Challenge group members to use their own creativity and apply their skill and experience sets to create something better in the community than already exists (new programs, new initiatives, new organizations).
- Increase collaboration with existing organizations that focus on sustainability targets of interest.
- Facilitate an educational exchange through the collective lessons learned by group members.

How to request sustainability coaching and speaking services?

email Ted Schierer at: tschierer@jettphc.com
- www.JohnMaxwellGroup.com/TedSchierer
- John Maxwell Company store with a full line of leadership products from John Maxwell
- Coaching assessments and forms
- Sustainability speaking services

EcoQuiz sustainability iPhone app
https://itunes.apple.com/us/app/ecoquiz/id422872829?
mt=8

JETT's first album, Tunnel Hill, features instrumental
mandolin and guitar music in thanksgiving to the Creator.

JETT music on Tunecore
http://www.tunecore.com/music/jett_sustainability

JETT music on iTunes
https://itunes.apple.com/us/album/tunnel-
hill/id580296157

JETT PHOTOGRAPHY
JETT nature photography features landscapes and close-
ups from across the United States.
http://jettphotography.zenfolio.com

www.ingramcontent.com/pod-product-compliance
Lightning Source LLC
Chambersburg PA
CBHW030836300326
41935CB00036B/177